Tales of a Community That Was...

Krassna · North Dakota
A Memoir

Written and Compiled by
Angeline Reinbold Ibarra

ElderBerry Books
CMP Publishing Group, LLC

Dedication

To our loving son John Jr. (Jack). 1973-2007 I greatly appreciated his encouragement as I began working on this book. Unfortunately he died in a work related accident and is not here to see its completion. His words of encouragement, "Go for it Mom," carried me through this project.

To my family
To my husband John for his love and support and the cover photograph.
To our son Graham for the chapter drawings, and to Philip, Peter and grandsons Kyle and Ryan for their emotional support.

This book is also dedicated to the early settlers of Krassna and to their descendants.
History shows these settler's created a bond to the land and to each other. Without their history this book could not have been written.

Angie Ibarra

Acknowledgments

I am grateful to the many people who have helped me make this book a reality.

A very special thanks to Edna Siniff for coming to my rescue when I was really in need of a publisher. I greatly appreciate the things she did, especially the attention to detail.

Allan Burke, a very very special thanks for granting permission to use the newspaper content.

Pasty Ramberg for her hours of proofreading and typing newspaper articles.

Albert (Al) & Alvina Ternes for drawing maps and providing aerial photographs and information.

Elsie (Pool) Ryckman for being my 4th grade teacher and supplying school information.

Jeff Flynn for helping to organize newspaper articles and photos.

Michael Miller for supplying G/R contact information.

A special thank you to the following people who have supplied photographs, information and support: August & Loretta (Braun) Vetter, Lorraine (Ternes) Bossert, Lavina (Schwab) Kaiser.

For the support of my extended family: Lawrence & Violet Reinbold, Keith & Johanna (Reinbold) Goebel- Larson.

A special thanks to the following people who have supported me with stories and encouragement. Bill Dykama, Sister Rosalind Gefre, Lorraine Gosewisch, Martha Haugen, Jaci Mitzel, Elizabeth (Reinbold) Ohanneson, Sister Rose Schwab and William Ternes.

Introduction

My original intention was to write a book only about the one-room school I attended.

Learning that DeKalb University in Illinois had a Program supporting Country Schools I decided to tell the story of Krassna schools in North Dakota. Using the DeKalb website I began my research. As I worked, I realized that I could not tell the story with out including the community and the everyday lives of the people who lived there.

"Tales of A Community That Was..." is the result of more than four years effort. This book shares the settlement of Krassna with the reader. The community of Krassna was settled by Germans from Russia in the late 1800s.

The farm on which I was born was settled and developed by my paternal grandparents, Ignatius and Barbara Wangler Reinbold. My family left Krassna when I was nine years old. This book covers the years from 1924 to the 1960s. It includes my memories and research, followed by newspaper articles to substantiate my writings.

Angie

Table of Contents

Prologue

Once there were three, then four, then five, then three and then there were none.

It was 1924 and three white clapboard school houses were opening to begin classes in a farming settlement called Krassna, North Dakota, located on dirt roads about ten miles from the little village of Strasburg.

A flicker tail gopher was looking at the surroundings before scampering into a hole, where he was perhaps going to hibernate for the winter. The meadowlarks were singing; my mother told me they were singing, "the house is made of gingerbread." The heat of the sun was warm and friendly on this October morning. The beautiful sun dogs were fading from the sky. However, the incessant wind was wiping across the barren hills and windswept prairie, blowing the tumble weeds. One rolled across the prairie and came to a complete stop in front of the steps of Schoolhouse #3.

The teachers were ringing the bells to summon the students from primary to grade eight, who were arriving either on foot or with horse and carriage. They were eager to attend school. The boys and girls were all descendents of Germans from Russia. Their parents and grandparents had arrived about 40 years earlier from The Steppes of Russia.

Besides the schools there was a white, clapboard Catholic Church with a cemetery close by. There was also a small store to meet the basic needs of the farming community. For other needs there was the village of Strasburg.

Now there are only memories.

NORTH DAKOTA HYMN

(Tune: Austrian Hymn)

North Dakota, North Dakota,
With thy prairies wide and free,
All thy sons and daughters love thee,
North Dakota, North Dakota,
Fairest state from sea to sea
North Dakota, North Dakota
Here we pledge ourselves to thee.

Hear thy loyal children singing,
Songs of happiness and praise,
Far and long the echoes ringing,
Through the vastness of thy ways-
North Dakota, North Dakota,
We will serve thee all our days.

Flag of North Dakota

Onward, onward, onward going,
 Light of courage in thine eyes,
Sweet the winds above thee blowing,
Green thy fields and fair thy skies,
 North Dakota North Dakota,
Brave the soul that in thee lies.

God of freedom, all victorious,
Give us souls serene and strong,
Strength to make the future glorious,
 Keep the echo of our song,
 North Dakota, North Dakota,
In our hearts forever long!

Written for Miss Minnie J. Nelson,
State Superintendent of Public Instruction, Watford city, October 18, 1926
James W. Foley

Maps

North Dakota

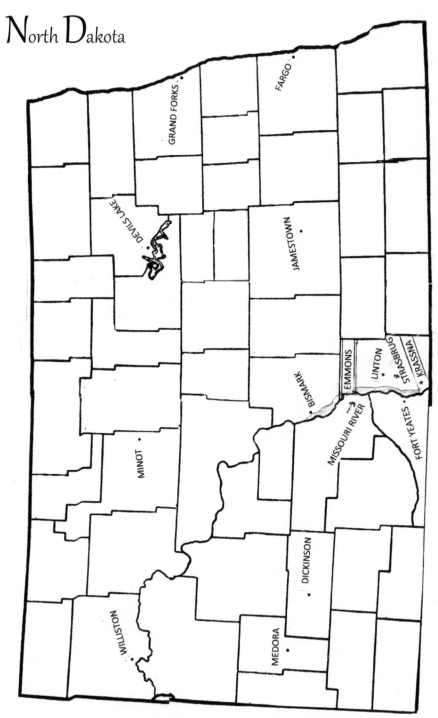

*The Missouri River is drawn to show only where
it was located in Emmons Country.*

Emmons County, North Dakota
Original School Districts

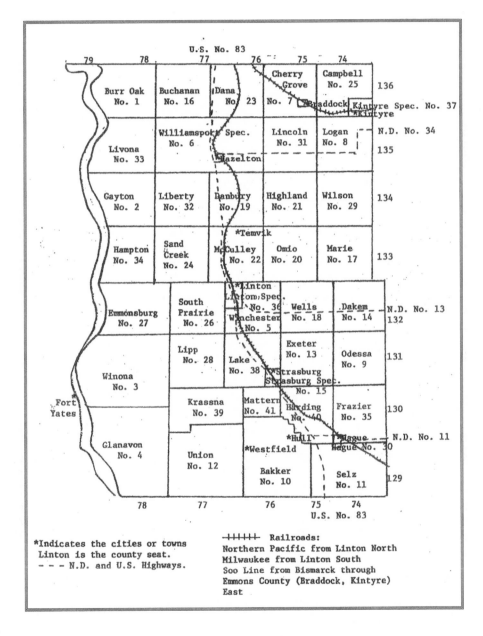

Krassna is No. 39 on the map.

Krassna, North Dakota

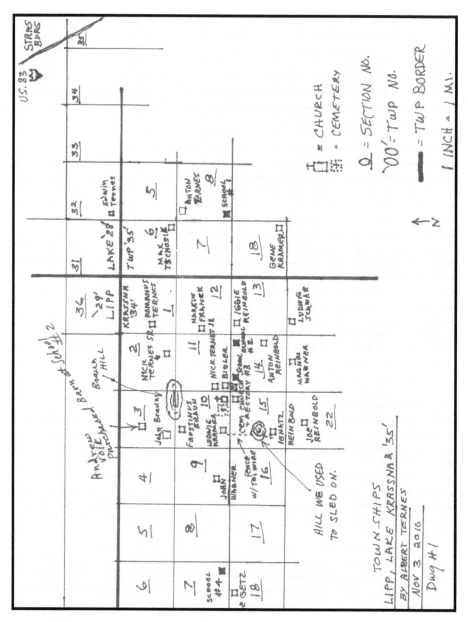

Enlargement of Krassna was drawn by Albert Ternes who also attended School No. 3. This map shows locations of Schools, family homes and points of interest to the residents and children of Krassna.

Early Settlers
The Other Germans

Angie's father Ignatius Reinbold
His parents were among the early settlers of Krassna.
Ignatius Reinbold, Sr.
Barbara Wangler-Reinbold

The Other Germans

A Brief History of The Early Settlers In Krassna, North Dakota

The people known as the Germans from Russia (G/R) were called "the other Germans" to distinguish them from Germans who emigrated directly from Germany. The Catholic G/Rs who settled in the community of Krassna have an interesting ancestry.

The G/R originated in Southern Germany. In the late 1700s they settled in Russia before migrating to the United States. While in Russia, these German Catholics settled in the colonies of Kurtchugen, a village now in the Ukraine. They also settled in Krassna, the only Catholic colony in Bessarabia, for which the North Dakota community was named.

The old Krassna is now in the Republic of Moldova. The place in Germany where our ancestors lived is now part of France, as the borders kept changing.

When Napoleon Bonaparte came to power in France, in the 1700s, he attacked his neighbors and eventually ruled all of mainland Europe. Germany was divided into many little kingdoms, therefore, he was able to march through Germany with ease because they could not unite for their common defense. He conquered the west bank of the Rhine forcing the Germans who lived there out of the country.

Our ancestors were among those who were forced to leave. They left Germany in the late 1700s, and early 1800s. As the saying goes, "when one door closes another one opens."

In 1763 Catherine the Great, a German princess, was now Czarina of Russia. She issued a manifesto offering very fertile land, known as the steppes of Russia, to the displaced Germans. Catherine the Great respected and admired the hard working ethics of the German farmers.

Czar Alexander I, the grandson of Catherine the Great, continued her policies.

In order to attract the Germans, the Russian government promised them land, financial support until the first crops were harvested, no taxes, no military duty, help with moving the families and other benefits. This was very inviting to the displaced Germans. They left Germany and traveled by ox cart caravans to the new land. It was a long and arduous trip taking many months. Some people did not survive the hardships along the way.

In Russia, life was very hard in the early years, many people died. Others grew homesick for their old life, or their families and friends, and returned to Germany.

The Germans in Russia remained in separate settlements and did not assimilate into the Russian culture. Their language, customs food ways, and religion remained exclusively German. Originally, they learned to live with their Russian neighbors but, time and bad experiences caused them to distrust all Russians, especially the officials and tax collectors. Over time, as their hard work made them increasingly successful, their Russian neighbors became envious of their success. The privileges given to them by Alexander I were revoked. Harsh taxes were imposed and the young German men were drafted into the Russian army. In 1876 the last of the rights granted to the Germans were revoked.

Life became so unbearable that leaving Russia seemed their only hope, but supposedly there was no place to go. Again another door was opened. During Lincoln's presidency the Homestead Act was passed. This opened a vast territory in the United States to immigrants who were willing to make the long and difficult journey to this country and try to survive on its great plains. These first settlers sent reports back to families and friends about the rich soil, the low cost of the land, and its vast prairies.

In 1889 North Dakota became a state. The officials of the State of North Dakota offered many perks to the settlers who were willing to relocate. Thus North Dakota ended up with approximately 23 percent of the German-Russian population in the United States.

Our ancestors settled in the south central area of North Dakota. This area is often referred to as the "Sauerkraut Triangle," but it is actually the shape of a polygon. The area they settled encompasses the counties of McIntosh, Emmons and Logan.

In Russia, the families lived in colonies and farmed the outlying areas surrounding the communities. In North Dakota they lived in separated farms, which the Homestead Act required. This made for a lonely existence for the early settlers. Krassna, located on dirt roads, made the families even more isolated as the roads were usually not drivable in the winter. Other hardships the settlers endured were the extreme cold in the winter and the heat in the summer.

The following resources are for those persons interested in learning more about the Germans from Russia.

American Historical Society of Germans from Russia, Lincoln NE
www.ahsgr.org

Center for Volga German Studies, Concordia University Library, Portland OR
www.cvgs.cu-portland.edu

Germans from Russia Heritage Collection, NDSU Libraries, Fargo ND
www.ndsu.edu/grhc

Germans from Russia Heritage Society, Bismarck ND
www.grhs.org

Glueckstal Colonies Research Association, Richmond VA
www.glueckstal.net

Sidney Heitman Germans from Russia Collection, Colorado State University Libraries, Fort Collins CO
http://library.colostate.edu/gfr

These resources are courtesy of North Dakota State University and were provided by Michael Miller.

Presidents of the United States 1923 to 1961

Calvin Coolidge,   Republican 1923-29
　　no Vice President, 1923-25
　　Charles G. Dawes, 1925-29
Herbert Clark Hoover,   Republican 1929-33
　　Charles Curtis
Franklin Delano Roosevelt,   Democratic 1933-45
　　John N. Garner,   1933-41
　　Henry A. Wallace,   1941-45
　　Harry S. Truman, 1945
Harry S. Truman,   Democratic 1945-53
　　no Vice President, 1945-49
　　Alben W. Barkley, 1949-53
Dwight David Eisenhower,   Republican 1953-61
　　Richard M. Nixon

KRASSNA SCHOOL DISTRICT
DATES OF OPERATION

Krassna School
　　#1 In operation from 1924-1952- burned in 1958
　　#2 In operation from 1924-1953
　　#3 In operation from 1924-1957
　　#4 In operation from 1926-1962
　　#5 In operation from 1936- 1940
　　　　Taught in Braun summer kitchen

The Krassna school district started in 1924. It included Lipp, Union and Strasburg district.

Schools

Class from School #5, taught in Braun's summer kitchen.
Photo courtesy of Loretta Braun Vetter

Schools

Never let schooling interfere with your education.

In 1924 the students from primary to the eighth-grade arrived at the schools to the sound of the ringing bells. Three little white school houses sat a few miles apart in a community of farms in an area called Krassna.

It was already cold for a fall day in October. School was just starting since Krassna had only seven months of school. Inside the potbelly stove was stoked with coal and wood by the teacher who had arrived earlier. It was too cold to shed coats, jackets and caps, so the cloakroom inside the front door was not used.

The white enameled water pail with the white dipper, trimmed in red, stood on a stand by the wall. On the front wall, to the right, was a built-in bookshelf with a small number of books. On the white painted wall to the left hung black and white portraits of George Washington and Abraham Lincoln. In the middle was a pull down U.S. and World Maps with names that seemed very foreign to the students who usually had not traveled out of Emmons County and never heard of the names, which were written in English.

The teacher's wooden desk was located under the map. Wooden desks were lined up to accommodate the students who ranged from five to around fifteen years of age. The desks had empty round holes for ink wells. One wall on the side was lined with windows that vibrated from the unceasing wind. On the south wall was a blackboard. In the southeast corner of the room stood the potbellied stove. At the back of the room was a book stand holding an enormous Webster's dictionary.

Outside there was a red barn where the horses for the students riding to school were kept. Next to the barn were two outdoor toilets, one for the boys and one for the girls with a Sears or Ward's catalog

Krassna School Number 3

for toilet paper. A flag pole rose next to the school house, with the flag standing straight out in the wind.

School, for me, started at age 5 when I started primary which is now called kindergarten. There was only one other student in my grade. While the teacher was teaching the other classes we could play or listen to what the teacher was teaching. It was a great setup because we were exposed to all the lessons from grade one to grade eight.

When I played at my desk I wanted to play with paper dolls. The other student at my desk, who was a male, wanted to play horses. So I ended up playing horses or playing by myself. I could also read one of the few books in the library. I loved the Dick & Jane books. I had never heard of anyone named either Dick or Jane. Most Krassna students had shades of brown hair and Dick and Jane had blond hair and their dad went to work in a suit. It was very foreign to me since I did not know any families who were like that.

Students would bring their lunch from home, usually in previously used syrup pails. Since the school was without ventilation the smells were not always pleasant. Lunch would usually consist of peanut butter sandwiches with syrup or honey. Sometimes sausage or canned chicken would be added. The garlic smell from the sausage would be particularly strong. Also the wool mittens drying on the stove would add to the olfactory senses along with the oiled saw dust floor.

We got apples at school which were given to North Dakota on the relief program during The Roosevelt Administration. Occasionally they also provided canned prunes. The teacher would heat the prunes on the pot bellied stove and students would have prunes for dessert at noon.

The students all knew each other. Everyone lived on surrounding farms. They were all descendents of G/Rs with German as their first language. The female teachers usually boarded with a nearby farm family. Several of our teachers were Dutch, which was our only diversity. According to the G/R they were The English. Anyone who was not a G/R was referred to as The English, no matter what their nationality. There was an imaginary line south of Krassna where the Dutch settled. The Dutch had settled earlier in North Dakota and had become more Americanized; therefore, they were available for teaching.

One of my first teachers was a man of Dutch descent who was married to a G/R Catholic. Every morning at the beginning of school we started out with a prayer. He said the prayer but did not make the sign of the cross, which seemed very strange to us Catholics, but he later converted and also ran for political offices. (He was a very nice teacher.) Two of the students from school number 3 went on to become teachers in the same school.

The parents expected their children to behave and expected the same from their teachers and other officials.

Following is a letter, written in broken English, by a parent to a teacher.

Dear Teacher

The kids came home tonight school and said that those (neighbor) kids and (cousins) were jumping the whole day long around the horses one of the horses is rolling around in the Barn and don't eat and is sick. Your are spose to tell those kids that they should quit it if not you shall tell their folks or Else we write the school supertented if they push the Buggy down the hill again you should give em a good spank. They should mind what you say if not the write the school supertendent and he should come and fix them.

...and if you don't train those kids better you will get kicked out of school house and pretty quick to

(With permission from the Institute of Regional Studies from the book "Plains Folk".)

Some of the students, and most of their parents, had Russian sounding names ending in "us" for boys. Common names were Pius,

Pederus, Faustinus, Eustachius, Magnus, Aloyus, Markus, Igantius or Nickolous.

The girl's names, most ending in "a," were Rosina, Johanna, Alvina, Cecilia, Christina, Narcissia, Regina, Philoppena, Elenora, Monica, Anna, Barbara and Martha.

Middle names, which became popular around the 1850s, had not yet reached the very rural area of Krassna. Since all the students attending the Krassna schools were Catholic, everyone was baptized with the name of a saint. Nick names were also popular to distinguish the people who had the same name.

We learned our ABCs, 123s, Civics, Geography, Arithmetic, Writing and Speaking English. We were mostly 1st and 2nd generation Germans from Russia. We had not heard of TV's or computers but we learned just the same, as for calculators, we used our fingers.

We learned how to speak English, thus becoming Americanized. One of the rules was that you had to speak English in school; recess, however was a different matter. If we were caught speaking German we had to write 100 times "I must not speak German in school." Being a creative group we would often use two or three pencils together so we could write two or three lines at once. I am sure the teacher knew what we were doing, but had other battles to pursue. Teaching the students English was not an easy task. The parents of the students did not know how to speak English, thus presenting a difficult task for the teacher. Everything in the community was conducted in German. Church services were in Latin, but sermons and songs were in German. North Dakota, in its exasperation to teach G/R kids to speak English eventually passed a law that everything relating to the school had to be communicated in English or they would lose funding. We were fast learners.

If you were disciplined in school you would also be disciplined at home, if your parents found out. Also, in the early years parents were limited financially and did not want to spend the money for paper for the kids to write "I will not speak German in school." So in order not to get into trouble students would go to the little country store nearby and get used wrapping paper to write on. If you had to stay after school, to write, you would be late arriving home to do your chores, so once again you would be in trouble.

Out in the desolated prairie, basics such as running water and electricity were still very futuristic. Water was transported from the nearest farm. If it was a cloudy day the school room would be dark, as we did not have lights in school.

Angie's Class in School #3

Creativity was our only means for fun as we had no playground equipment or any other toys at school. Recess was a big event. Everyone usually played together, as everyone was needed. Sometimes students played soft ball or kitten ball as the game was called, using a stick for a bat and whatever could be found for a ball.

Another game similar to hockey was called piggy. Each player had a wooden stick and there were small holes dug in the ground, one less hole than players. A can was placed in the middle; the object of the game was to knock the can away. The one player without a hole had to go and knock the can back, trying to get the can to touch one of the players with their sticks in their respective holes.

Other times the boys played marbles, while the girls played jacks, or everyone would play Fox and Goose, Ring around the Rosy, Andy-Andy Over and many other games depending on the season.

We were not always the best-behaved students. Sometimes we would all run away to the next school, which was about a mile away, usually to play baseball, while the teacher was inside preparing lessons. The teacher would be ringing the bell after recess and no students would show up. I don't remember what we got for punishment.

Another mischievous thing we did was smoke. One time someone brought real cigarettes to school. Other times we would pick weeds resembling tobacco, which grew in the school yard and roll our cigarettes with tablet paper. My first experience with smoking was that I did not know how to inhale. I blew into the rolled tablet paper and it started on fire. Not knowing what to do I threw it into the trash can, which also started on fire. Fortunately, that is as far as it went. My smoking days were limited. I usually tell people I started smoking when I was 6 and quit when I was 7.

*Angie and Lawrence's pony and cart that
provided their transportation to school.*

My brother and I had a Shetland pony with a little cart that we used to drive to school. If I threatened to tell my parents what we did, like smoking, my brother would drive over all the hills on the way home scaring the daylights out of me, so I never told.

Some forms of punishment used by the teacher, if a student really misbehaved, was to have them hold the big Webster's Dictionary with arms outstretched. Kneeling on coal or corn was another form of punishment. One of the earlier teachers believed that if one student misbehaved all should be punished. They would have to line up to get wacked. The boys caught on quick and put handkerchiefs in their pockets. Don't know what the girls did as I was not yet attending school. Although, we were mischievous we did not misbehave big time very often and hardly ever duplicated the behavior.

North Dakota allowed schools to be held in non-school buildings, if there were enough students and a teacher was available. One such school, School #5 was held in a summer kitchen. One of the students who preferred to do other things rather then go to class would let a mean buck sheep out of the pen just before the teacher, who was boarding with the family, stepped out of the house to enter the summer kitchen. When the buck chased her she would run back into the house. Class was either delayed or the teacher would not come out for the rest of the day. After a few such incidents the parents put a stop to that trick.

The students had daily duties to perform each school day. The flag was put out every day and taken in and folded at the end of each school day. The black board erasers were cleaned each Friday by clapping them together enveloping the student and surrounding area with a cloud of white chalk dust.

Attending high school in the earlier years was not a common practice. The nearest high school was in Strasburg. Unless you had grandparents or other relatives that you could stay with there was no way you could attend school, especially in the winter time when the roads were closed. However, most students became successful even with just a few years of education. The boys learned farming from their dads and the girls learned housekeeping and child rearing from their mothers. Some students also became business people. They learned early on how to figure things out and usually succeeded.

Reinbold School, Krassna School #2.
Photo Courtesy of Lavina Schwab Kaiser.

Angie Ibarra

EMMONS COUNTY RECORD

OFFICIAL NEWSPAPER OF EMMONS COUNTY AND CITY OF LINTON

1922

CAMPAIGN TO WIPE OUT ILLITERACY IN EMMONS COUNTY

Many are responding promptly to our letter in regarding names and addresses of all illiterates. We hope all will report at once, even if there are no illiterates; as we wish to begin our campaign as soon as we possibly can. Superintendent Woll has agreed to help us all he can and we feel that this is going to be a banner year in wiping out illiteracy in Emmons County. Our main work from now on is going to be the diminishing of illiteracy in the county. We are working without a field deputy but will endeavor to make a visit to every school desiring our help in teaching illiterates. We intend to clean up this County this winter if possible. It will prove an added burden upon this office, however, if it is necessary to make added sacrifices. We intend to do our best.

We hope teachers will not look upon this matter as a way to make extra money. If you cannot get enough students to comply with the law relative to receiving part of the state aid, if your district refuses to pay anything on that account we hope you will regard the matter as a duty and an opportunity to do service to mankind. We realize the job is liable to be a thankless one in many instances, but one illiterate taught to read and write will be a source of boundless as something other to yourself.

We in the offices are willing to teach illiterates who will present themselves to us. Will you not do what you can? Your efforts will broaden you as a teacher and make you feel that you really are doing something. If you have any illiterates and they will not attend school go to their home and gain their confidence and get them to allow you to help them at home. If you have several in your locality try and get them to some neighbors home, or if you cannot do that visit each home one or two nights a week.

We want no illiteracy after this year. Let us put Emmons County on the map, as being the first county to clean up illiteracy. The ministers of the United States are cooperating with educators and the American Legion is making "American Education week" December 8 a success. We hope all ministers in the county will devote a sermon or part of a sermon on December 3 to *Continue on next page*

28

EMMONS COUNTY RECORD

Continued from previous page

education. This office will furnish them with any facts they may desire. A letter will go out to every minister this week requesting his cooperation. If we miss only one please do not feel slighted as we do not know all. We also are getting out a letter to each teacher in the county we want them to get every parent to visit school at least twice.

1923
WHY FATHER SENDS SON TO "DAKOTA"

He worked for the Standard Oil Company many years. He knew that his firm preferred office help from Dakota Business College, Fargo North Dakota. That nearly 700 banks in the biggest wholesalers employ DBC graduates "a good school for my boy," Mr. Reinhold decided Sequel. Young John Reinhold is now with Standard Oil's Fargo branch, the 12th DBC student placed there. Let your sons and daughters follow the successful. Summer classes are less crowded pupil's advance faster, and earn money sooner.

7-23-1923
KRASSNA
"DAKOTANS "MAKE GOOD ANYWHERE

Graduates of Dakota Business College, Fargo, North Dakota are so thoroughly grounded in the theories and practices of modern business that they easily hold their own wherever they go. Ethel Walker wintering in Los Angeles got a position at the Chevrolet auto company the first week. Gilbert Olson has accepted a fine situation with the Sunburst (Mont) State Bank.

7-23-1924
KRASSNA
NIGHT SCHOOLS MAKE BIG GAINS

Enrollment in night schools throughout the state has grown from 1750 in 1921 to 2755 at the end of 1922. Forty-nine night schools cooperating in the campaign for "No Illiteracy in North Dakota in 1924" have an average enrollment of 94 persons.

EMMONS COUNTY RECORD

7-23-1923
KRASSNA

PRECAUTIONS TO PREVENT ILLNESS

When school opens in the fall all children that have been playing or working out of doors should be watched rather carefully. The change from a day of physical activities to one of seven or more hours of confinement is great and may bring on illnesses unless a few precautions are taken. For a short time at least the school day might well be broken up into more than the usual number of periods and the children given frequent recesses. They should be advised to eat less hardly of strong foods during the first two weeks of school so that the physical machine considerably slowed down as it is, may have a chance to adjust itself.

More over the first assembling of large number of children from different homes may mean bringing in the germs of colds, measles, scarlet fever or other diseases. Proper foresight on the part of authorities can nearly always keep these from being epidemic. The school should be the most healthful place we have for children.

7-23-1925
KRASSNA

4,285 SCHOOL CHILDREN

There are 4,285 school children in Emmons County, according to H.H. Hanson county superintendent of schools. The girls lead with 2,295 and there are 1989 boys. This is a big increase over the previous year according to Mr. Hanson

EMMONS COUNTY RECORD

7-23-1926
KRASSNA

KRASSNA SCHOOL NOTES

H.H. Hanson Supt. of schools of Emmons County visited our school last Thursday and we were all very glad to see him.

Cecilla Ternes started to school last Monday. Joe Schmaltz treated our school barn to a new coat of paint. The color being red.

Father Eichner pastor of the Catholic Church here has catechism at the school house every week on Tuesdays and Fridays from four o'clock until four-thirty

Ludwig Kramer hauled a load of coal to our school Tuesday.

Mary Holzer started to school last Monday.

Ida Ternes was absent from school on Monday as she was bothered with an ear-ache.

Pius Kramer was absent from school on account of sickness.

Bessie Morgan, Teacher.

The fourth grade is learning the poem "The Letter Home", for language.

We spent a part of the time last Friday after last recess in having a "geographical match." The fourth fifth sixth and seventh grades taking part in it. The pupils all seemed to take great interest in this and insist on having another one soon.

1926

STATE LIBRARY COMMISSION ISSUES LIST OF BOOKS SUITABLE FOR GIFTS.

Below is a partial list of recommended books

Several hundred volumes are contained in the list of books which the state library commission this year is recommending to prospective purchasers of Christmas gifts.

The list, according to Miss. Lillian Cook, state librarian is intended for use by persons who are forced to buy hurriedly and who might otherwise have little knowledge of what is good or bad for the person to whom they intend to present the volume. It is also intended as an indication to bookstores and stationers of the type of volume which librarians are recommending to the public.

Commenting on the problems of book buying Miss Cook said, "In buying books avoid books in series written by one author about the same person or group of persons. Buy books with good physical makeup, especially clear and

Continued on next page

EMMONS COUNTY RECORD

Continued from previous page

large print. Buy books which are strong and sane in morals, correct in grammar and construction, truthful in the lessons they teach and wholesome in viewpoint.

Anyone who has book buying problems which this list does not solve is cordially urged to write to the state library commission in regard to individual problems and suggestions will gladly be given for adult books as well as books for juveniles.

Order your books through your local bookstore or write to the state library commission as to where to get the most quickly and economically. Let this be a book Christmas for all the family but be sure they are books worth giving and worth accepting as friends

None of the books recommended by the library commission costs more than one dollar.

The list of books recommended for small children follows. The title of the book name of the author, name of the publisher and price are given in order.

Children's Books

Little Black Sambo, Hellen Bannerman, Stokes, $.75

The story of a little black boy whose wonderful shoes took him into the jungle where he helped the tiger become, "the grandest in all the jungle."

Old Mother West Wind, T. W., Burgeas, ,$1.

A story telling the adventures of the merry little breezes released daily. Good bedtime reading. Also Mother West Wind's How Stories, Mother West Wind's Animal Friends and Mother West Wind's Children. Same publisher and price

Peter Rabbit, Beatrix Potter, Warne $.75

Five Little Peppers, Margaret Sidney, Lethrop, $.60

Stories of Fairy, Wonder and Myth Land

The Arabian Nights published by Winston, $.80

Alice's Adventure in Wonderland, Lewis Carroll, Winston $.80

Pinocchio C. Colodi, Winston $.80

The capers of a wooden marionette.

The Wonder Book and Tangle-wood Tales, Nathanial Hawthorne, published by Jacobs's contains two volumes.

Poetry

Sing Song, Christina Rosetti, McMillan $.75- A nursery rhyme book

Child's Garden of Verses, R. L. Stevenson Rand $.75

Stories of Heroes Real and Legendary

Story of My Life, Helen Keller, Grosset $.75

Letters of Theodore Roosevelt to His Children, Scribners $1.00

Some Merry Adventures of Robin Hood, Howard Pyle's Scribners $.76

Continued on next page

EMMONS COUNTY RECORD

Continued from previous page

Stories Recommended by Miss. Cook for Children before the Teen Age are:

Hans Brinker M.M. Dodge, Grosset $.75. A picture of life in Holland

Dog of Flanders, Louise de la Ramee, Bryce $.90 .A Christmas story of old Antwerp.

Heidi, Johanna Spyri

Boy's Stories

Tom Sawyer, S.L. Clemens, Modern Classic Edition Harper $1.00

Stories for Girls

Little Women, A. M. Alcott, Winston $.88. One of the best girls stories ever written.

7-23-1927

KRASSNA

COUNTY SCHOOL NOTES

By Curtis Jenkins

As a result of the teachers examination in February eight applicants received certificates. Those securing second-grade elementary certificates were Catherine Harvey, Pauline Flegele, Mrs. Gertrude Holm, Esther L. Klaudt, Bert R. Hagan, Doris Phillips and Audrey Fogle. Leonard Jellema received a first elementary.

Hampton school district has given its teachers a month of additional time lengthening the term to eight months. That is very pleasing to this office.

The county superintendent attended a very successful P.T.A. meeting in union district last Friday evening. Although the house was packed with nearly 200 people, excellent order prevailed. A very good program was enjoyed by all. While the lunch was being prepared, a number of amusing stunts were done; the writer was drawn for a "crawling- through- the- hoop- contest and almost caused his side to lose because the hoop was too small for the purpose. Anyway we enjoyed the evening very much.

Miss. Margaret Piedt has finished her term in Winona and is completing one in Lipp. Ruth Haedblad of Louise Grunfelder's school in Wilson was neither absent or tardy during the term just closed, which entitles her to a beautiful certificate of perfect attendance.

Schools were visited in Bakker, Clanavon, McCulley, and Lincoln last week.

The school at Temvik gave a home talent play last Friday evening to raise money to get playground equipment. We hope to see every school supplied with a good assortment of playground and athletic equipment in the near future. Good manly sports besides being good exercise, solves a big amount of disciplinary troubles.

EMMONS COUNTY RECORD

7-23-1927
KRASSNA
COMMUNITY SCHOOL NOTES
FACTS REGARDING SCHOOL ACTIVITIES
By Curtis Jenkins

As most of the schools are now in session we are beginning our school notes with this issue of your paper. We shall try to make our notes cover school activities for the whole county. And we shall try to make them of interest to teachers, patrons, school boards and pupils.

Practically all our teachers are engaged, and we think it is a strong corps of teachers which have been secured for the coming year to trust with the mental, moral and physical development of our school children. Practically all of our teachers have had some normal training. Many have completed the Standard Normal course for two years. It pleases us to learn several of these are teaching in one-room rural schools.

Non-attendance reports coming in from many schools are very discouraging. Some schools where there were twenty five or thirty pupils last year, opened this year with one or two pupils enrolled, and in one or two cases, none. In two cases we know of seven-year-old pupils were kept out of school to work. School is by far the most important activity of child life, and parents as well as teachers, should make the pupil feel that everything else is subordinate to his acquiring an education. Keeping children out of school to work is surely not the way to create interest in school for the pupil. There is one opportune time to get an education, and if a person fails to secure an education then the chances are a hundred to one that he will never get one. No permits to keep children out will be recommended for pupils under thirteen years of age, or for those over that age who are under grade. For pupils over thirteen years of age, a short time permit will be recommended when the conditions seem to warrant it. But in any case, it is a misdemeanor to keep a pupil out without a permit. Enforcing the compulsory attendance law is one of the many duties of this office. It is often an unpleasant duty for some people resent having anyone tell them to send their children to school.

Teachers should notify this office the day school opens. We will then send them Notice of Beginning School blanks. These should be filled out and sent to this office as soon as possible.

There are several clerks who have not

Continued on next page

Continued from previous page

sent us their Teacher's Contracts yet. I wish to urge them to do so at once. We must have them on file in this office.

We have supplements to the State Course of Study in Literature. There is a charge of twenty cents each for them.

Now, this is the beginning of another term of school. We can make it just as good or poor as we choose. If patrons and school boards will join me in pulling with the teacher we can put across a successful term of school in every class room in the county. If there are failures let us not lay too much blame upon the teacher, as we are pretty much, if not equally responsible, for the failure. Let us boost work, and succeed together.

7-23-1927
KRASSNA

N.D. STUDENTS MUST LEARN GOOD ENGLISH

North Dakota high school students will hereafter be taught not to say "He don't" or "I done," and that all sentences begin with a capital letter, in preference to who wrote Il Penseroso which was the greatest of the Shakespearean dramas, according to an announcement from the state department of public instruction.

The department has at last decided that it is more important for a high school student to be able to speak and write his mother tongue than to be able to quote long passages from the classics or state Milton's favorite color.

Teachers of English in the schools throughout the state are to be asked to cooperate in this "back to nature" movement in the course of study and will study grammar more than famous works from now on. The reason for the changes, according to officials, is the result of a recent survey which showed students to be much lacking in fundamental English.

EMMONS COUNTY RECORD

7-23-1928

KRASSNA

N.D. EDUCATIONAL ASS'N TO MEET
EMMONS COUNTY SCHOOL NOTES
PLAY GROUND EQUIPMENT NEEDED

By Curtis Jenkins

The North Dakota Educational association meeting is to be held at Bismarck October 26, 27 and 28. This promises to be a very successful meeting. Much time and effort have been given to preparing a program. We believe school boards should excuse teachers who want to attend this meeting. It may be several years before the state meeting is held so close to our county again.

The following schools have sent in their enrollment fees to the Junior Red Cross.

Highland No 1, Lois Wallace, teacher

Hampton 1, Margaret Piedt

Livona 4, W. S. Hembecker

Union 1, Nina Putnam

Wilson 2 Louise Grunefelder

Lipp 1, Jeanette Wimmer

Gayton 4, Mabelle Walhood

Emmonsburg 1, Hilda A. Knudtson

Emmonsburg 4, Esther Klaudt

Selz 1, Mrs. Evelyn Schatz

Winnifred Mandigo is substitute teacher for her sister, Ethel during the latter's illness.

The visiting teacher will be here October 29th to Nov. 4th. We will not be able to visit all our schools. We hope all the schools will be flying the flag by then. The general appearance of many schools could be greatly improved by hauling away ash piles, mowing the lawns, etc.

We would be delighted to see every school in this county well provided with playground equipment. Bending over work tends to make a pupil hollow chested, round shouldered, etc. Giant strides chinning bars, trapeze rings are all good playground equipment for correcting these ill effects as well as such games as volley ball and basket ball. A student needs the stretching up exercises.

#13 1928

elpful
ousehold
ints

DIET OF THE SCHOOL CHILD

With the opening of the city and country schools the past two weeks mothers, no doubt, are giving extra time, thought and attention to the preparation of proper foods for their children, who are attending school. The interested and thinking mother realizes that her children will be better able to concentrate on their lessons at school and that their whole attitude towards school tasks will be more alert and receptive, if their little bodies are well-nourished with the right kind of food. A healthy body makes a healthy mind -a healthy mind makes an active brain- an active brain makes a brilliant student. So therefore, it is well for every mother to be mindful of her school child's diet, that he may derive the most benefit from his school year.

What Children Need for Growth

For perfect development of body and mind, certain fundamental physical conditions are required. Among these are pure air, food and water, warmth and protection, sleep and rest, freedom and exercise. It is therefore wise to surround children with these conditions which are most favorable to healthy growth.

The following rules may be used as a guide to promote health:

A full bath at least twice a week.

Brushing the teeth at least once a day, preferably evening

Sleeping long hours with windows open.

Drinking as much milk as possible not less than one pint, but no tea or coffee.

Eating some vegetables or food every day.

Drinking at least four glasses of water a day.

Playing part of every day outdoors.

A bowel movement every day.

The Right Foods for Children—

A child's meal should never be selected from one or two articles; a variety of foods is needed to furnish all kinds of growing materials. At the same time monotony in food is overcome. Every day the mother should see that her child's diet contains some of each of the following types of food.

Milk-is the best and most important food for growing children. There is no substitute. It is the most perfect food we have. It is also one of the least expensive foods. Milk is a good fuel because it contains fat and sugar. The body

Continued on next page

EMMONS COUNTY RECORD

Continued from previous page

needs fuel to keep it warm and to make it move and work and play, just as the steam engine needs coal or the automobile needs gasoline. You should know where your milk supply comes from and how it is inspected.

At least a pint of milk a day (not more than a quart) should be included in the daily diet of every child.

When a child dislikes to drink milk alone give him his share in the form of cocoa, custards, milk soups, creamed dishes, etc.

Eggs, Fish Meat-If plenty of milk and an egg a day are selected for the diet of the child, very little meat should be given before the seventh or eight year. The broth from stews may be given with crackers or bread or served on vegetables. Serve the eggs soft-boiled poached or hard-boiled, but avoid fried eggs as the frying in hot grease tends to toughen the albumin in the white making it difficult for digestion.

Cereals and Other Grain Products- these foodstuffs should supply at least one third of the food requirements of a child. Cereals and flours containing the outside of the grain- such as graham, whole wheat and rice are more nourishing than the refined cereals in flours because they contain special life-giving factors called vitamins. They also help to prevent constipation.

If children do not like cereals it is usually because the cereals have not been properly cooked. Cereals must be cooked for three hours over boiling water. This thorough cooking makes the starch more digestible.

Vegetables are a very important factor in the diet. They are essential in guarding against constipation.

Potatoes should be given practically every day in some form, such as baked, boiled, creamed or mashed.

Other valuable vegetables are peas and beans, spinach, string beans, squash, celery, asparagus, carrots and beets, either fresh, dried or canned. Green vegetables are particularly rich in Iron and vitamins.

Fruit— a child should have some fruit in the diet every day. Where fresh food is not possible dried foods may be used. Dried foods also have rich iron content. Fresh food should be given in season whenever possible. All fruits should be wiped off with a damp cloth before being eaten, including apples.

Sweets should never be given between meals. They should be given in the foodstuffs such as cocoa, puddings, custards, fruits, etc. or at the end of a meal. Candy or sweets offered at the close of the meal may often be used as an enticement for a child to eat well of the main foods of the meal.

Fat— This is essential for growing children. Milk fat is the most important kind. See that they use generous servings of cream in there cereals, puddings etc. Fats and sugars and starches (carbohydrates) are the greatest sources of energy. Avoid fried foods.

Continued on next page

EMMONS COUNTY RECORD

Continued from previous page

In general summary— If your child receives his correct portions of milk, eggs, cereals, vegetables, fruits, fats and sweets in balanced ration, and gets plenty of rest and fresh air, he will without doubt, grow to be healthy in body, mind and spirit and be a credit to his school, home and community. Mothers be mindful of the health of our future citizens

---

March 28, 1929

EMMONS COUNTY SCHOOL NOTES

By Supt. Jenkins

SOME 7 MONTH SCHOOLS HAVE CLOSED-TOO SHORT SAYS COUNTY SUPT.

Several of the schools with seven month terms have closed. This impresses us with the fact that a seven months term is too short. Every town school in the county has a nine-month term. The country children need an education just as much as the town children. In fairness to the rural boys and girls they too should have the advantages of a long-term. We hope that all the rural districts will soon see the many advantages of a nine-month term and adopt it. Below is a list of all the rural districts with the length of their school term.

The following rural districts have nine months: Buchanan, Dana, Campbell, Lincoln, Danbury, Highland, Sand Creek, McCulley, Union and Baker.

The following districts have eight month schools: Burr Oakes, Lavona, Logan, Gayton, Wilson, Omio, Glanavon Devine and Harding.

The following districts have seven month schools: Hampton, Marie, South Prairie, Winchester, Wells, Dakem, Winona, Lipp, Lake, Exeter, Odessa, Krassna, Frazer, and Selz.

The following districts have mixed terms of seven, eight and nine months. Cherry Grove, Liberty and Emmonsburg.

Eight grade examinations will occur May 27, 28, and 29. High school examinations will be conducted May 24, 27, 28, 29, and 31.

The following pupils of Herbert Folson's school in Wells had perfect attendance for the last half of the term and were given perfect attendance awards: Andrew and Elizabeth Klein

EMMONS COUNTY RECORD

March 19, 1931

LAWS RELATING TO EDUCATION PASSED
TEACHER QUALIFICATIONS TO BE RAISED
INCREASE IN H.S. TUITION

The last Legislature passed twenty-three laws relating to education in a greater or less degree. Most of these measures were of minor importance and will not be mentioned here. However, three of these laws are important since they affect schools, especially rural districts, in a direct way. A brief discussion of each is offered below.

House Bill 127

Raises qualifications for teachers. Under the present law a high school graduate may be granted a teaching certificate upon completion of 12 weeks of normal training. The new law, which goes into effect next September 1, requires one year of normal training. This will not affect this year's high school graduates who wish to take training and qualify to teach before the law goes into effect.

House Bill 74

Increases high school tuition. At the present time a school district without a high school must pay tuition for pupils from its' district who attend high school in some other district. The present law sets six dollars per month or fifty four per year as the amount. The new law increases tuition to eight dollars per month or seventy- two dollars per year. This may work a hardship upon some rural districts which have a considerable number of pupils attending high school outside the district.

Senate Bill 112

Increases the minimum length of school term. At present it is contrary to law for a district to have less than a seven month term. The new law increases this to eight. Thirty-one of our forty-one districts now have a longer than a seven month term. It is not thought this increase will work any considerable hardship on any districts, as those such as Burr Oak, Livona, Gayton and Glanavon which have lowest assessed valuations, small enrollment per school, pay considerable tuition, transportation, etc. already have eight and nine month terms.

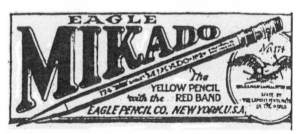

EMMONS COUNTY RECORD

1934

COUNTY SCHOOL NOTES
By Co. Supt. Curtis Jenkins

The third Friday in January is designated by law as "Temperance Day." This year the date is January 19. It is required that every public school in North Dakota shall devote at least one hour to appropriate instruction and exercises relative to the benefits of temperance. A number of schools will give temperance programs and others will give a period to instruction.

Ninety-one teachers are conducting seventh and eighth grade examinations Thursday and Friday of this week. The tests are for completion. A student who has done a full year's work in a subject is eligible to write. The Examinations are not trial tests for just anyone who happens to be in one of these grades. Since elementary education is by far the most important phase of the educative ladder, we want to feel sure that a pupil is well grounded in the grade subjects before he is given a diploma of graduation. A student is seriously handicapped in high school and college unless he has received a good common school education. A very good state examination is now being offered and any applicant who can pass the test with good marks is ready to quit grade school work and will have little trouble in doing high school work.

The scrubbing and sterilizing of school houses, project carried on during the holidays has been completed and was quite successful. Practically all labor was paid by the health service of the CWA.

EMMONS COUNTY RECORD

3-22-1934

NURSES INSPECTING SCHOOL CHILDREN COUNTY ORGANIZED WITH ELLA BECK AND MARY FISCHER AS INSPECTORS

By Curtis Jenkins

For a long time we have sought to have the school children of the county given a health inspection. Now our wishes have been realized. Acting suddenly upon a petition presented by the local board of health, the CWS sent a field worker down and organized the work for the county. Ella Beck of Linton and Mary Fischer of Strasburg were selected to do the work. These two well qualified nurses are now busy inspecting

Rules and regulations have just gone out to rural schools the children in the seven-month schools. As soon as the short-term schools are inspected, work will be continued in the long-term ones. This service is paid for entirely, both salary and mileage by the federal government and deserves a one hundred percent cooperation on the part of parents and teachers

However, we wish to point out that the fact that an inspection will do little good unless something is for the singing and declamation exercises. Dates have not yet been set. Play done for the pupils who are found to be defective. It will do little good to find that a child has decaying teeth or weak eyesight unless something is done about it. Therefore, we urge every parent who can possibly do so to have the physical defects corrected as soon as possible after being informed what they are. For those children whose parents are unable to have the necessary work done, a health fund should be set aside.

day regulations have also been sent out.

EMMONS COUNTY RECORD

9-1934

First Supt. of Schools Sends Greetings to All Old Friends

Hon. John H. Worst Says Greatest Difficulty in Establishing Schools Was to Secure Trained Teachers

Editor's Note-Mr. Worst is one of Emmons county's most outstanding pioneer citizens. Besides being its first superintendent of schools he preached, taught Sunday school was the main speaker at nearly every public gathering and officiated at many early-day weddings. He was state senator from this district for several years and later became president of the North Dakota Agricultural College, which position he held until he retired a few years ago. He now lies with his son on a ranch in McKenzie County.

EMMONS COUNTY RECORD

5-14-1936

THE IDEAL STUDENT

An ideal student is one who has as few faults as possible and is still a human being. The ideal student is one who spends his vacant periods studying, not using them as recreation periods. He takes part in school activities and is a good sport at all times. The student that lets his head swell to abnormal size because he has done some extra good work falls short of being an ideal student.

Some pupils, boys especially go to school only to get into high school athletics. Others go to spend their time annoying teachers and their classmates. If each student would try to do everything and not overdo any one thing, I am sure that any student body would be a happier, better unified and more efficient group.

5-14-1936

COUNTY SCHOOL NOTES

By Curtis Jenkins

Our participation in the state Young Citizens League convention at Bismarck was well covered in the local paper last week, but we want to take this opportunity to express our thanks to the teachers for their efforts in getting the delegates to Bismarck and to the delegates for their excellent behavior while attending the meeting. Also, we wish to congratulate Vern McCulley upon the successful candidacy for state vice president of the YCL.

To the senior officers of the YCL and to the teachers and pupils of the sixty three schools which organized units, go our thanks. It was their interest and enthusiasm that made the work in this county worthwhile.

Extended term to nine months

Recently Sand Creek extended its term from a seven to a nine-month term. This leaves only two short-term districts in the north half of the county. They are Marie and Wilson, Marie will most likely change to an eight-month term next year.

Extension of their term was considered, but financial problems prevented. Several seven month terms were extended.

Below are listed the districts and the length term maintained

7 Month Term

Districts Winona, Winchester, Dakem, Marie, Wells, South Prairie, Emmonsburg, Wilson, Frazier, Krassna.

8 Month Term Districts

Glanavon, Logan, Selz, Exeter, Omio, Dana, Lipp, Hampton, Lake, Harding, Gayton.

EMMONS COUNTY RECORD

9-24-1936

OFFER HIGH SCHOOL TRAINING TO ALL
DISABILITY NO BAR TO PUPIL. COUNTY SUPT. CURTIS JENKINS SAYS

The opportunity to secure high school training is now open to every young person in Emmons County. Those who are unable to attend regular high schools because of financial conditions or physical disabilities will be considered for enrollment in supervised high school correspondence subjects.

Under this high school plan, pupils are allowed to attend their rural schools and study correspondence courses at no expense except for cost of books, postage on lessons and one dollar registration fee per subject.

Disabled persons may receive permission to study their correspondence lessons at home; all others must study their lessons in a rural or a town school.

Subjects offered are English 1,2,3 and 4, public speaking, elementary algebra, business arithmetic, geometry, general science, biology, astronomy, healthful living, world history, U.S. history, economics, commercial law, Junior business training, typewriting ,shorthand, bookkeeping, beginning art, show- card writing, food study, clothing construction, poultry husbandry, feeding farm animals, and gas engines.

Last year only a few Emmons pupils enrolled for a correspondence course, County Superintendent Curtis Jenkins says but this year already eight or ten have applied and many more are expected.

One important feature Mr. Jenkins points out is that pupils attending regular high schools may enroll in correspondence courses in subjects not offered by their high schools, providing the correspondence subjects are made a part of the students regular school work under supervision of one of the teachers. For instance, if a pupil is unable to enroll in bookkeeping, typewriting, diesel engineering, etc. in regular classes he may apply thru his teacher for an enrollment blank.

Any person unable to attend regular high school classes should write to Mr. Jenkins for further information about this method of enrolling in high school work.

EMMONS COUNTY RECORD

6-3-1937

SCHOOL SURVEY TO START THIS MONTH
EMMONS AMONG 31 COUNTIES TO BE CHECKED FOR EDUCATIONAL DATA

A federal sponsored survey of North Dakota school problems in 31 counties in which Emmons is included is expected to begin June 15 at the Grand Forks University under the direction of Dr. A. V. Overn.

The survey will seek educational data on school district organization in the state, and will present its findings to the governor and Legislature.

Investigations already completed or underway in 22 counties reveal that North Dakota has more school board members than teachers. In contrast to most states, North Dakota Board members receive salaries. It is pointed out.

Another problem is that small school districts often result in the rural child tho living as little as a half mile from a city school, being forced to walk as much as 2 miles to a one- room school. Because of transportation facilities and lack of proper financing, the average rural child does not have the educational opportunities available in the cities.

In addition school teacher salaries in different parts of the state vary more than 400 per cent.

The trend during the past 25 years says Dr. Overn, "has been to intensify the weakness of the present North Dakota public school system."

Graduates students, usually local superintendents working for advanced degrees have already completed or are continuing to study in 22 counties.

Among the 31 counties to be included in the survey are: Emmons, Logan, Sioux and McIntosh.

7-22-1937

EMMONS HAS 4,475 OF SCHOOL AGE
CENSUS REVEALS OVER THIRD OF COUNTY POPULATION BETWEEN 6 AND 21

A report just completed by County Superintendent Curtis Jenkins reveals that Emmons County has 4475 persons of school age. Based on figures from the 1930 federal census, this shows that over one third of the county's population is comprised of school age persons.

1939

CORRESPONDENCE SCHOOL PLAN RECEIVES NATIONAL ATTENTION

Country Gentleman Publishes Article About NDAC Supervised Study Course

North Dakota's progress in the development of correspondence study is receiving nationwide attention as a result of an article entitled "North Dakota solves a school problem" in the November issue of Country Gentleman, national farm magazine.

Written by T. W. Thordarson, the article tells of the striking growth of the supervised correspondence study project in this state.

Designed to "remove some of the disadvantages that stood in the way of the farm boy and girl" the North Dakota correspondence study plan aids three classes of young people -the rural student, who once unable to pursue high school studies, now takes high school work by mail under the supervision of rural teachers; the disabled child, who can study under the supervision of family members; and the regular high school student who along with standard high school work can now broaden his education by taking special studies under the correspondence project.

Thordarson directs the extensive project from the study center established at the North Dakota Agricultural College at Fargo. Here 25 specialists give their attention to the problem of rural students.

The first year the correspondence set-up was established 2000 young people enrolled in 25 subjects. Last year the projects had 5000 students enrolled in 49 subjects. This year an enrollment of 6000 is expected.

Fifty North Dakota high schools used the service last year now more than 300 of the state's 500 high schools act as agencies for advancing their world youth education.

Emphasizing that the plan although termed supervised places complete responsibility on the individual, the work is described by Thordarson as a part of progressive education, in which every enrolled person is on his own to study at his own rate. He is taught to study by himself and to test his own capabilities.

4-19-1941

EMMONS COUNTY RECORD

4/22-1942

COUNTY SCHOOL NOTES
By Supt. J. D. Moriarty

I am taking this opportunity to call upon the teachers of the county to announce a great cause, The Victory Garden. This cause will bring us closer to that final victory. With the shortage of tin it will mean a shortage of commercial canned goods the coming year. Too offset this more vegetables must be raised and canned at home. It can be done so let us do it.

The home garden in many cases can be carried on by the children themselves. All we need to do is arouse the interest of them for raising a garden and with the teachers and parents help they will do it. Children take pride in their work. So once more let us show the people of Emmons County who they can rely upon to accomplish difficult tasks. Every home needs and should have a victory Garden.

May I urge young people and more used –to- be- teachers to write the teachers' examinations this month. We will need more teachers next fall. We must almost entirely depend on our own people to teach our schools. There was only one examination held each year, the last Thursday or Friday of April. Each applicant must be 18 years of age and pay a fee of $2.00. This is set by law and cannot be changed.

NOTICE OF TEACHERS EXAMINATIONS

Notice is hereby given that the annual teachers examinations will be given in Emmons County on Thursday and Friday, April 24 and 25 1941, in the courthouse in Linton beginning at 830 o'clock each morning. This will be the only examination this year.

Age and citizenship are the only qualifications for applicants. An applicant must be a citizen and eighteen years of age on or before the date of the examinations. There will be a fee of $2.00. Examination paper and ink will be furnished.

Applicants are asked to file their names at the county superintendent's office by the 21st so sufficient examination papers may be secured.

J. D. MORIARTY,
Co. Supt. of Schools,
Emmons County N.D.

April 17 – 24

EMMONS COUNTY RECORD

September 9, 1943

BOARD APPOINTS SUPT. OF SCHOOLS

Philippine Baumgartner assumes County office, deputy announced later

Miss. Philippine Baumgartner, Deputy Superintendent of Schools, was appointed to fill out the term of J. D. Moriarty, re-signed by the County commissioners as they met at the courthouse Wednesday afternoon. She assumed duties immediately.

That Miss Baumgartner can capably fill the duties of her office is shown by her long record of service in the county office. Serving as deputy superintendent under C. B. Jenkins for five years she was appointed to fill out his term in 1940 when he re-signed to accept the secretaryship of the draft board. For the past three years she has served as deputy for J. D. Moriarty.

Previous to her office work, she taught in Eaxter and Harding districts near Strasburg and at Valley City. Philippine is a graduate of the Strasburg high school and Valley City teachers College. Appointment of a deputy will be made at a later day, she advises.

Philippine Baumgartner Berglund

Candidate for

County Superintendent of Schools

Emmons County, N. Dak.

YOUR VOTE WILL BE APPRECIATED

(Sponsored and Paid for by Philippine Baumgartner Berglund)

Philippine Berglund, Superintendent of Emmons County retired in 1974. She died Nov. 5, 2005 at age 95. Here husband Gus died in 1974

49

EMMONS COUNTY RECORD

1943

STATE CALLS FOR MORE TEACHERS
SPECIAL EXAMINATION WILL BE HELD HERE ON OCTOBER 5 AND 6

The State Department of public instruction has issued a call for more teachers to fill vacancies in North Dakota rural schools and to meet the need will hold a special teachers' examination in most counties the forepart of October.

Complying with the request, and to supply a need for qualified instructors in Emmons schools County Superintendent J. D. Moriarty announces that a special examination for applicants for second-grade elementary teachers 'certificates will be held in Linton on October 5 and 6.

The examination is open to all applicants who are citizens and over 18 years of age. It includes everyone teaching without a certificate, who must write the examination. It will also be necessary for those persons who have received extensions of their certificates, or whose extensions are in progress, to write the examinations.

The office said Monday that Emmons schools are short about 40 teachers, including those who are teaching without certificates.

It is expected that between 50 and 60 applicants will write the examination. Logan County last week was short 43 teachers.

As a result of the examination Emmons school boards should be provided with a list of qualified teachers whom they can employee and thus make their districts eligible for state aid, the office said.

The examinations will be held in the Memorial Hall of the courthouse starting at 9 a.m. each day.

January 4, 1945

Philippine Baumgartner weds Lt. Berglund

Announcements were received in Linton this week telling of the marriage in St. Augustine Florida of Miss Philippine Baumgartner of Linton and Lt. G. H. Berglund army. The wedding was read in St. Augustine on December 23. The bride is superintendent of Emmons County schools and has been visiting in Florida for about a month. Lt. Berglund's home is in Carrington North Dakota. Mrs. Berglund's mother is Mrs. Michael Baumgartner of Strasburg. We have no further details.

EMMONS COUNTY RECORD

September 9, 1948

COUNTY LEADS IN TEACHER SHORTAGE
60 POSITIONS VACANT AS OF AUGUST 31, SOME FILLED SINCE SURVEY

According to a story published in the Fargo Forum last Sunday, Emmons County led all counties in the state in shortage of schoolteachers. A statewide survey conducted by the Forum at that time revealed that Emmons County was short 60 teachers.

Every county in the state reported teachers needed. Dunn County was second to Emmons with 55 short, and Kidder and Mercer needed 45.

Philippine B. Berglund, Emmons County Superintendent of schools, said Wednesday the situation has eased somewhat since the Forum survey was made. She said a number of teachers have returned contracts since that time. She added however, that at least 40 vacancies still exist.

Mrs. Berglund said the condition is not unusual and is encountered every fall in recent years. She said many teachers hold back contracts until the last possible minute. The superintendent also said many schools now without teachers will find applicants before Oct. 1.

Nevertheless, Mrs. Berglund said the teacher situation in the county, as in the rest of the state, is serious. Last year 29 schools in the county remained closed throughout the year. The reason in almost every case was inability to hire teachers.

Asked the reason for the widespread shortage of teachers, Mrs. Berglund listed several. She said unsatisfactory salaries leads the list despite substantial increases during the past three years.

Emmons County teachers received an average monthly raise last year amounting to almost $24. Increases had been granted the previous year also. Another reason cited by Mrs. Berglund is housing and living conditions encountered. Young

Continued on next page

Angie's first teacher

51

Continued from previous page

people she said do not care to experience the rigors of rural life in North Dakota, especially in winter. They prefer to enter work which will allow them the comparative comfort of town living.

Transportation and roads also are factors in the shortage of teachers, Mrs. Berglund said. Many districts in which roads are blocked a good share of the winter months find it difficult to attract teachers.

Mrs. Berglund said although the situation in Emmons County is not now as desperate as when the Forum made its survey, it still is serious.

The superintendent added that continued shortage of teachers is bound to lower educational standards in the county

---

5-5-1949

EMMONS COUNTY PLAY DAYS SCHEDULED FOR MAY 11 AND 12

Hundreds of schoolchildren from throughout Emmons County will gather at Seeman Park, next week, Wednesday and Thursday for the annual County Play Days. The town kids will compete in athletic events on May 11th, the rural kids on May 12th. Mrs. Philippine Berglund, Co. Supt. of schools will be in charge. G. A. Berglund will manage the town program and Matt Wangler the rural program.

Mrs. Berglund asks all schools to arrange and bring picnic lunches and to assemble at the park at 10:30 a.m.

The athletic events for boys and girls will start promptly at 4:30 in the afternoon of each day. Ribbons will be awarded to winners of first second and third places in each event.

Alvin Tschosik ran for County Superintendent June 1958.

EMMONS COUNTY RECORD

1950

TEACHING STANDARDS Of ONE ROOM SCHOOLS DOWN

A recently completed survey of teachers in one room schools in North Dakota shows the number of such schools is declining and teacher qualifications are improving.

M.F. Peterson state superintendent of public instruction said there are 2,572 certified teachers in one room schools and 469 who are not certified. This compares with 2616, certified last year and 651 who were not certified.

Peterson is of the opinion that since there are fewer one-room schools, some of the smaller enrollment schools are closing and sending their pupils to larger schools.

There are 6800 grade and high school teachers in North Dakota at the present time

August 20, 1950

SCHOOLS STARTING AGE REMAINS SAME THIS YEAR

Those parents who are wondering whether their children are old enough to start school this year are reminded that the law passed by the legislature at its 1959 session made no changes for this year.

The law as passed last winter makes no changes for 1959; therefore children who are six by Dec. 31 may start school at the beginning of the term in September.

There will however be changes for 1960 and 1961. Next year children must be six years old by Nov. 30 and in 1961 and thereafter they must be six by Oct. 31st.

The new law is particularly important to those parents who wish to start their children in kindergarten. If the parents are not careful in picking the correct time, the children may wind up spending two years in kindergarten or one year in kindergarten, then one year at home before starting the first the first grade.

EMMONS COUNTY RECORD

December 14, 1950

BILL TO EDUCATE UNUSUAL CHILDREN GETS APPROVAL

Action by the North Dakota legislative research committee at a meeting in Bismarck last week included:

Approvals of a proposed bill to provide for education of exceptional children, such as are unable to benefit from the regular public education facilities.

As proposed to the researchers by the state Department of public instructions, the measure would include a $50,000 appropriation to instate the start of the program.

The committee will continue its meeting this week.

1951

THE ONLY CHANCE REHABILITATION IS POLICY OFF FLORENCE CRITTENTON HOME

So quietly and discretely that you may seldom realize its existence is the way a North Dakota service has been working wonders with tragic young lives.

To thousands of unmarried mothers and their babies, the Florence Crittenton home of Fargo has meant a chance to rebuild their lives. It has been the difference between despair and the opportunity to find useful, normal lives.

A few individuals have generously furnished physical facilities for this refuge over its 50 year history in Fargo.

Who are these girls? The girls helped at the Florence Crittenton home have one thing in common -each is in desperate need of help because she is to bear a child without being married. She needs physical, mental and spiritual help.

In most cases she can see only black disaster and terror ahead. She is confused and frightened.

Condemnations, scorn and desertion could result in suicide or fatal abortion attempts unless some help is found.

Also, most of the girls are very young- only a few years older than one of them who brought her doll; she was 12. In other respects they are completely varied as to race, religion, economic status and family background. No girl is refused help. The Florence Crittenton Home is none- sectarian.

Continued on next page

Continued from previous page

Every girl is given spiritual assistance, attends the church of her choice and the Home works closely with the clergy of all faiths. In many cases, girls are told about the Home by their religious leader whom they go to for advice. Others come through various charitable groups, through doctors or lawyers, or through friends.

They are not "bad" girls they are people who made a mistake that could wreck their lives and the lives of their babies were not wise counsel and practical aid given.

What is done for the girls? They are given through and competent medical care, including prenatal hospital delivery and postnatal -care. This maternity care is provided through the cooperation of St. John's Hospital at Fargo, where a nominal charge is made if the girl or her family is in a position to pay.

Up to the limits of present space, girls live in a Home for approximately three months while every possible help is given in working out the problems involved. This help concentrates upon developing in the girl a healthy, hopeful approach to her future and the future of her baby. The situation at home, the relationship and the responsible man, and economic problem are investigated and analyzed as to the best course of action. In the planning and case work, the services and cooperation of all other appropriate agencies are fully utilized.

Counseling and education fill individual needs. Training in home nursing and home economics are part of it. In many cases a chance to finish grade and high school requirements is of great importance. In others, help in finding a job solves most urgent requirements.

All these are given in the most friendly and sympathetic way. When a girl leaves the Home, she is better equipped physically mentally and emotionally for responsible citizenship.

EMMONS COUNTY RECORD

December 4, 1952

70 PERCENT OF NORTH DAKOTA STUDENTS FINISH SCHOOL

High schools in the state are now being attended by 70% of the students who finished the grades according to Richard K. Klein director of the secondary education division in the state superintendent's office.

Klein spoke at the annual conference of the North Dakota Council on education pointing out that half a century ago, North Dakota high schools were attended only by about 11 per cent of those students who finished grade school. The questions confronted today by those planning high school courses, according to Klein, is still much the same as it was in the early days.

"Shall we design for the 70 percent who now normally attend or should we try to make high school curricula so attractive that 100 per cent of the grade school graduates will continue through the 12th grade?"

Klein produced figures-based on interviews with 440 boys and girls who quit in the upper grades or high school- to show that more than 47 per cent of them dropped out because of dissatisfaction with school.

Seventy-four said they just plain failed grades, while 29 said they did so because of discouragement or did not like the courses. 25 more didn't like their teachers or teaching methods.

Klein said of all who quit school for various reasons 19 per cent said they did so because of economic need.

Klein told the council he believed that if secondary education is to be for all -rather than the select college preparatory core group- the high school courses of study should be made 100 per cent attractive.

Efforts to this end he said should include making instructions and the course of instruction so varied that every student can find courses in which he is interested and which he will find of practical benefit.

1952
SISTERS IN 12 SCHOOLS TO DON MODERN DRESSES

About 60 of the 74 nuns teaching last year will don civilian dresses so they can continue teaching in public schools in North Dakota this year, a recent survey shows.

In the primary election last June, voters of North Dakota approved an initiated act to prohibit public-school teachers from wearing garb denoting membership in any religious order. The measure passed by a margin of 11,500 votes.

Sisters will continue to teach in civilian dress in 12 of the 19 public schools where they taught last year. Five of the 19 schools are converting to parochial Catholic schools, thus losing public tax support. In two communities this means converting just one room in an otherwise all-parochial school.

The sisters are quitting as teachers at two schools Gladstone and Olga.

Schools where sisters will continue to teach in civilian dresses are Callo, Selz, Lefor, South Heart, Leahy, District 4, Mt. Carmel, Hague, Strasburg, Richardton, Karlsruhe and Balta.

The five Schools converting from public to Catholic schools are at Mantador, St. Pius, Wild Rice, Oakwood and Haymarch, the latter in the Wehrl district.

September 24, 1953
NO TEACHING VACANCIES IN COUNTY RURAL SCHOOLS

Unlike other years, all Emmons County rural schools were able to open on schedule this year. All schools had teachers signed up for the 1953-54 term, says Mrs. Philippine Berglund, County Superintendent of schools.

Two weeks before school opens Mrs. Berglund added the teacher situation looked worse than it has in the past number of years.

Mrs. Berglund also expressed pleasure at the large number of rural schools which had been painted and cleaned this year. She estimated that over half of them had been put into good shape for opening day

EMMONS COUNTY RECORD

August 30 1956

RURAL TEACHERS NEEDED IN COUNTY

With the school term almost ready to begin, Emmons County is still short many rural teachers, according to Mrs. Philippine Berglund County Superintendent of schools. She estimates that 30 or more teachers can still find employment in the county. According to reports from the various school boards the shortage is much greater, but many boards have hired their teachers and have so far failed to report.

As far as is known, all the town and city schools in the county have hired complete slates of instructors.

Salaries for rural teachers in the county range from $180 to $225 per month for those who are certified $150 to $175 for does not certified

September 12, 1957

TWO TEACHERS LEAVE; ASKED BETTER FACILITIES

Another problem which may become serious in the future appeared in Emmons County last week.

Two prospective rural school teachers, who arrived here Thursday, were on their way back home Saturday because they were not satisfied with living conditions on local farms. They wanted to stay at a farm that had telephone service and running water.

Although many Emmons farms are very modern, there are still many which do not have telephone service, nor modern plumbing facilities. Available teachers for rural schools are scarce and in the future excellent living conditions may figure in their choice of positions, as well as the amount of the salary offered.

As of early this week Emmons County was still short about 15 teachers for rural schools.

March 15, 1958

LIGHTNING FIRES SCHOOL SOUTHWEST OF STRASBURG

During the heavy electrical storm in southern Emmons County Monday evening lightning set fire to the Bichler school about 6 miles southwest of Strasburg in Krassna District.

The fire destroyed the entire building which had been unused since the spring of 1952 and continued nothing of great value. The school is located near the Max Tschosik farm now occupied by his son Peter.

EMMONS COUNTY RECORD

September 8, 1959

47 ATTEND FIRST SESSION OF ADULT FARM SCHOOL

The first session of this year's adult farm school drew 47 farmers says Roland Okerstrom, vocational agriculture instructor at Linton Public High School. He added that many of the farmers' wives attended the course for the ladies, conducted by Mrs. Kenneth Meier of the school's home economics department.

Guest speaker at the first session was Clark Monroe, superintendent of the state Highway Patrol who talked on the legal rights of the farmer on the highway.

The farm school classes will be held each Monday evening at the Linton school until Dec. 7.

Mr. Okerstrom reminds all those who may be interested that the school is absolutely free and that all farmers are invited to attend any or all of the sessions.

C. B. JENKINS RETIRES AS ASCO
WOULD—BE CANADIAN SERVES HERE 32 YEARS

In the summer of 1914 a young man left his home in Indiana with the intentions of following the harvest from Kansas northward into Canada. It was his ambition to file on a homestead, then enlist in the Canadian army to fight overseas in World War I.

On Monday, November 2 of this year that same man will not show up at his office in the Emmons County Courthouse. He didn't make it to Canada -- and is just now winding up 32 years of service in this county, all of which found him going to the courthouse nearly every working day in carrying out his duties.

Curtis B. (Curt) Jenkins has decided to "hang up his pencil" and retire from his position as office manager of the Emmons County ASC (Agricultural Stabilization and Conservation) Committee, a position he has held since 1946. He submitted his resignation a month ago to become effective on Nov. 1.

Before that he was secretary of the Selective Board, county Superintendent of schools, a rural school teacher and a school board director.

Mr. Jenkins was born at Marengo, Ind. attended grade and high school there and then went on to Central Normal a teachers college at Danville, Ind. This prepared him for a career as a teacher and he taught for a time in Indiana. Then came

Continued on next page

Continued from previous page

the beginning of World War 1 in Europe (1914 and his ambitions to become a Canadian homesteader and soldier began to take form.)

First he went to Kansas to work in the harvest fields. As the season progressed, he went northward arriving at the Tom Shea farm near Hazelton in time for the harvest. He remained in that area for several years, making the Shea farms his headquarters. During this time he taught in the two-room consolidated school near the Goughnour farm in Buchanan District.

In July 1917, he enlisted in the army saw service overseas and attended the AEF (American Expeditionary Forces) University at Beaune, France. This was an experiment in education combining academic and military studies which attracted many of the foremost educators of this country. He was discharged in August, 1920 and returned to Hazelton and his teaching position.

His dreams of homesteading in Canada were discarded completely in 1921 when he married Miss Helen Peery at Hazelton. She was a teacher too, so they both taught in the Buchanan schools.

In 1926 Mr. Jenkins entered county politics and was elected county superintendent of schools, succeeding Henry Hansen. He held the position for almost 14 years resigning in November 1940 to become secretary of the Emmons County Selective Service Board. This position he held until the spring of 1946 when he resigned and became fieldsman with the old PME (Production Marketing Administration) Mrs. Grace Anderson resigned as secretary of that setup in 1947 and he was appointed to succeed her. The term "secretary" was later dropped and the position became known as "office manager" several years ago PMA became ASC.

Beside his many years of service in public office he was commander of the Dan R. Richardson post of the American Legion in 1929, post adjutant in 1930, state Americanism chairman in 1938 -39, 5th district deputy commander 1940- 41 and post service officer for 14 years.

He maintained an active interest in education over the years, serving as a member of the Linton Special School District board for 12 years. He chose not to run for re-election in 1958.

As a member of the Linton Masonic Lodge which he joined in 1916, he has held almost every office serving as Worshipful Master in 1932.

Mr. and Mrs. Jenkins now live on their farm on the western outskirts of

Continued on next page

EMMONS COUNTY RECORD

Continued from previous page

Linton. Their two sons have completed college and are now holding responsible positions elsewhere. Mrs. Jenkins who served as deputy county superintendent for her husband and later for Mrs. Berglund is now teaching her third term in the Temvik school.

Mr. Jenkins immediate intentions are to devote his time to his farm and to enjoy his retirement.

Curtis Jenkins died March 1970, Helen died December 1985.

September 3, 1959

NEW STUDENT AGE LAW CLARIFIED BY BURGUM

In an effort to clarify the new law concerning how old a pupil must be before he or she may legally quit school, Attorney General Leslie R. Burgum has pointed out some of his main points.

The effect of the new law is to require school attendance if a child has not finished the 8th grade only until the child is 16. The old law required attendance until 17.

The law reads: "Every parent, guardian, or other person who resides in any school district and has control over any educable child of an age of seven years to sixteen years shall send or take the child to public school each year during, the entire time the public schools of the district are in session."

October 1959

ADULT FARM SCHOOL TO FEATURE WIDE VARIETY OF SUBJECTS

The annual adult farmers' evening school, scheduled to begin here Monday evening Oct. 5, promises a wide variety and useful range of subjects, says Roland Okerstrom vocational agriculture instructor at Linton public high school.

Subjects for discussion at the weekly sessions were selected by an advisory board consisting of County agent Ben Barrett, John Dosch, Joe Kalberer, Ray Kramer, Verl Mausehund, Dave Miller, Ray Splonskowski and Wilbur Vander Vorst.

Wives of the farmers attending the school have not been forgotten. While their husbands are at the school, the wives will be holding their own classes in the school's home-economics department under the direction of Mrs. K. A. Meier home economics instructor.

Continued on next page

EMMONS COUNTY RECORD

Continued from previous page

The ladies will study "Tricks of the Trade."

The evening school will continue its regular Monday evening sessions to Nov. 30 and will then be climaxed with the regular banquet on Monday evening, Dec. 7. Gov. John E. Davis will be the principal speaker.

All those who attend three or more meetings are eligible to attend the banquet.

Monday evening's session should be of particular interest to all farmers, Clark Monroe, superintendent of the state Highway Patrol, will discuss Legal Rights of a Farmer on a Highway.

On the following Mondays, the subjects will be (in that order): Tillage and Rotation Practices; Experiment Stations and the Extension Service; Balanced Rations; Farm Liability; Dwarfism in cattle; Pastures; Feeding Value of Grain and Roughage; Shelter Belts. Special speakers have been engaged for several of the above sessions.

The classes will begin each Monday evening at 8 p.m... To make it possible to cover all the subjects, one Thursday evening class will be held October 29.

As in other years, the school this year is again sponsored by the vocational agriculture department of the Linton Public High School. Advertising and the banquet are underwritten by the Linton Civic Club.

November 5, 1959

EMMONS GIVES $5,552 FOR 2862 SCHOOLCHILDREN

The first appointment of state tuition funds for the current school year was announced this week by Peterson, state superintendent of public instruction.

Emmons County's share of the apportionment is $5,552 based on a total of 2,862 school children in this county.

Apportionment for the entire state is $341,917 for a total of 176,246 children. This amounts to $1.94 for each school child.

Mr. Peterson's announcement stated that there has been a total increase in school age population of 7,685 since the 1957 school census.

Funds for the deportment are derived from interest and income from bonds representing money invested, rents from use of school land, lease money and bonuses from school land, fines and penalties. Money from the sale of school land is not distributed but becomes a part of the permanent common school fund.

EMMONS COUNTY RECORD

October 12, 1959

SCHOOL CHILDREN UNDER 16 MUST STAY IN SCHOOL

The use of children under 16 years of age for agricultural work is permitted under federal law, "only when school is not in session," according Sen. Milton R. Young at Washington.

In a telephone conversation with the Senator, Garfield B. Nordstrom superintendent of the North Dakota department of instruction was told that Young had so advised the North Dakota Farm Bureau. These are the provisions of the amended Fair Labor Standards Act, passed by Congress, which is now in effect.

The federal law does not supersede North Dakota child labor laws, compulsory school attendance laws, or the powers and duties of school board officials. Young is said to have pointed out, it merely supplements these laws, he said.

"Laws of this nature," Young said, "are for the prevention of the exploitation of children."

The senator continued, "The citizens of North Dakota have always been jealous guardians of the school privileges and opportunities provided for their children."

He emphasized that farm employers are also responsible for the observation of the federal standards as well as state laws which reinforce school attendance laws.

1959

ONE ROOM SCHOOLS CUT FROM 103 TO 55 IN 10 –YEAR PERIOD

Figures released last week by M. F. Peterson, state superintendent of public instruction, show that Emmons County has gone along with the remainder of the state in generally reducing the number of one-room rural schools in operation.

Mr. Peterson's statistics show that in the 1949-50 school year 103 one room rural schools were in operation in Emmons. This year 1959- 60 only 55 are being used. The latter figure represents a reduction of 10 since 1958-59 school year.

The state as a whole showed a reduction from 2689 in 1949-50 to 1106 in 1950- 60- or more than half.

Reorganization appears to be the biggest reason behind the shift away from one room schools.

Continued on next page

EMMONS COUNTY RECORD

Continued from previous page

Peterson called reorganization one of the major means by which education can be improved.

He listed the following as advantages of reorganization more nearly equal educational opportunity for children, higher degree of uniformity of school tax rates among districts, wiser use of public funds appropriated for education, more effective and efficient use of teachers equipment and facilities.

Mr. Peterson also said that despite the reduction in number of schools and school districts, the demand for teachers has gone up instead of down. He attributed this to increased enrollment.

Alone with reorganization have come higher standards for teachers.

"At the moment we know of no unqualified teachers employed in the schools; three years ago there were 419 Peterson said.

HIGHER EDUCATION

Not so many years ago one could count on the fingers of his two hands the number of Emmons County young people who went on to college. Now it would take a lot of hands with a lot of fingers.

We have received news from the University of North Dakota, at Grand Forks and the Valley City Teachers College, telling of the number of students from each county enrolled. The University lists 17 from Emmons and VCSTC 21.

The number at other colleges are rather large numbers for careers in an age when education is practically an absolute necessity.

1964

SCHOOL GROUP SETS DISSOLUTION HEARINGS, JULY 27

In accordance with state law, the Emmons County Committee for reorganization of School Districts has set a hearing at which dissolution or annexation of several districts will be discussed and considered.

The hearings will be held at the courthouse in Linton Monday night July 27.

Up for consideration will be the future of Exeter, Lake and Mattern districts, in the immediate vicinity of Strasburg; Krassna District, Winona

Continued on next page

Continued from previous page

District, west of Linton and Strasburg, and Gayton District southwest of Hazleton.

These have not operated a school in the past two years. The law requires such hearings for districts which have not operated schools in the immediate past two years. It does not apply to districts which border on another state which send pupils to schools in the state on which they border.

1966
SCHOOL PLAN APPROVED BY 218 -- 88 VOTE

The proposal to re-organize a number of school districts in the Strasburg area into one large district was given the go-ahead at the election held Tuesday of this week by total vote of 218 to 88.

In the rural areas it was approved by a vote of 129 to 7. In Strasburg the vote was 89 to 81 in favor. For approval the plan had to carry in both the city and rural areas.

The vote at the various polling places was as follows:

Rural Unit	YES	NO
Winona	15	0
Exeter	28	1
Lipp	10	0
Lake	40	0
Krassna	19	0
Harding	12	1
Mattern	5	5
Total	129	7
Strasburg Unit	89	81
Grand Total	218	88

The new unit will be known as Strasburg Public School District. Before this plan was approved, the district had 2 ¾ sections with a total taxable valuation of $1,309,305.

Next step will be an election to be held in about a month, at which a new school board will be named.

Selected Teachers Reports   Krassna, North Dakota

School Year 1924-25

SUMMARY OF ENROLLMENT AND ATTENDANCE

a. Enrollment: Boys _13_ Girls _10_ Total _23_
City boys _0_ City girls _0_ Total _0_
Farm boys _13_ Farm girls _10_ Total _23_
No. enrolled in 1st grade _7_ In 2nd grade _5_ In 3rd grade _4_ In 4th grade _0_ In 5th grade _5_ In 6th grade _2_ In 7th grade _—_ In 8th grade _✓_.
No. pupils enrolled in high school
(above eighth grade) - - - Total _—_
City boys _—_ City girls _—_ Total _—_
Farm boys _—_ Farm girls _—_ Total _—_
No. pupils completing 8th grade - - _✓_
City boys _____ City girls _____ Total_____
Farm boys _____ Farm girls _____ Total_____
No. pupils completing high school (12th grade) - - - - - - - _✓_
City boys _____ City girls _____ Total_____
Farm boys _____ Farm girls _____ Total_____
b. No. days school was taught (All days for which pay will be received) - - _140_
c. Aggregate days of teaching - - _3220_
d. Aggregate attendance - - _2091¼_ _2891¼_
e. *Aggregate absence - - - _326⅞_
f. **Aggregate non-membership - - _822⅞_
g. Average daily attendance (d ÷ b) - _14.93_
h. Per cent of attendance d ÷ (d+e) - _87.2_
Verification: See that d plus e plus f equals c.
Also that a times b equals c.

1. No. visits of county superintendent - _1_
2. No. visits of deputy superintendent - _____
3. No. visits of school officers - - _1_
4. No. other visits - - - - _1_

1. No. books in library, (not including text books) - - - - - _56_
2. No. books per pupil per grade in library _2+_
3. No. books purchased this year - - - _0_
4. No. loaned this year - - - - _0_

No. months school was taught, including all legal holidays and other days for which pay will be received - - _7_
No. of actual days of teaching (exclude holidays) - - - - - _125_
Salary of teacher per month - - - _85_
Grades taught - - - - - - _5_
No. Classes taught per day - - _25_ _28_

Is there a U. S. flag in your school? - _Yes_
Do you use it as required by law? - _✓_

*"Absence" means illegal non-attendance.
**"Non-membership" means legal non-attendance.

TEACHER'S REPORT

School No. _1_
of _Krassna_ School District No. _39_
County of _Emmons_, State of North Dakota

County Superintendent of Schools:
I hereby submit my report for the term beginning _Sept. 29,_ _1924_, and ending _April 10,_ _1925_
Francis M. Brittain Teacher
Dated at _Strasburg, No Dak._ _4/10_ 192 _5_

Duplicate sent to clerk _4/16_ 192 _5_
Report received _4/16_ 192 _5_

GENERAL STATEMENT

A. Teacher's Training and Experience - -
1. No. years completed above 8th grade _4_
Where _Geland, No Dak_ When _1923_
_____Co. Supt.
Graduate Normal School _No_
Where _____ When_____
Graduate college or university _No_
Where_____ When_____
2. No. years' experience _2_
Country _2_ City _2_
3. Are you a member of the State Educational Association? _Yes_
4. Are you a member of the N. E. A.? _No_
B. School Property
Repairs and supplies needed: _Flagstaff_
Gen. repairs on Bldg.
Fountain towels
C. Community Center Activities
Have you in your school district:
(a) A Farmers' Club? _✓_
(b) A Parent-Teacher Organization? _Yes_
(c) A Boys' and Girls' Club? _✓_
2. How many school entertainments (not held in school hours)? _3_
D. Health Conservation
Have you in your school:
(a) Hot noon lunch? _No_
(b) Medical inspection by nurse? _No_
By doctor? _No_
(c) No. individuals inspected? _✓_
(d) No. individuals having defects? _✓_
(e) No. individuals having defects remedied? _____
(f) How many times was your school-room floor scrubbed this term? _2_
E. Is your school standardized for aid? _No_

Daily Program and Classification
1924

9:00 - 15 Opening Ex.
9:15 - 10 Beginners Read.
9:25 - 10 First Reading
9:35 - 10 Second "
9:45 - 10 Third "
9:55 - 10 Fifth Reading
10:05 - 05 Sixth "
10:10 - 20 Third a. Arith.
10:30 - 15 Recess.
10:45 - 20 Sixth Arith.
11:05 - 00 Fifth Arith.
11:25 - 15 Third B Arith.
11:40 - 10 Second Arith.
11:50 - 10 First Arith.
12:00 - 1:15 noon.
1:15 - 15 Study Period.
1:30 - 15 Fifth Geography.
1:45 - 15 Sixth "
2:00 - 10 Phonics
2:10 - 10 First Reading
2:20 - 15 Physiology.
2:35 - 10 Second Reading
2:45 - 15 Recess
3:00 - 10 Third Geography
3:10 - 20 Language
3:30 - 05 First Spelling
3:35 - 05 Second "
3:40 - 05 Third "
3:45 - 05 Fifth + Sixth "
3:50 - 10 Penmanship
4:00 Dismissal

School Year 1941-42

TEACHER'S REPORT

School No. *3*

of *Krassna* .... School District No. *39*

County of *Emmons*, State of North Dakota

To County Superintendent of Schools:
I hereby submit my report for the term beginning *September 22nd*, 1941, and ending *May 1*, 1942

Ernest Born .... Teacher

Dated at *May 8* 1942

Duplicate sent to clerk .... *5 - 13* 19 *42*

Report received .... *5 - 13* 19 *42*

A. Moriarty .... Co. Supt. *73*

GENERAL STATEMENT

A. Teacher's Training and Experience:
1. No. years completed above H. S. *two*
   Where *Iowa* .... When *1930*
   Graduate Normal School *yes*
   Where *Cella, Iowa* .... When *1930*
   Graduate college or university *Central College*
   Where .... When ....
2. No. years' experience *five*
   Country *two* .... City *three*
3. Number and Kind of Certificate *1st Grade Elem.*
4. Are you a member of the State Educational Association? ....
5. Are you a member of the N. E. A.? ....

B. School Property:
   Repairs and supplies needed: *Globe - play*
   ground equipment - swings - seesaw.

C. Community Center Activites
1. Have you in your school district:
   (a) A Parent-Teacher Organization? ....
   (b) A Farmers' Club? ....
   (c) A Boys' and Girls' Club? ....
   (d) Young Citizens' League Organizations? *Yes*
2. How many school entertainments (not held in school hours)? *one*

D. Health Conservation
   Have you in your school:
   (a) Hot noon lunch? *no*
      (1) Surplus commodities *yes*
      (2) Other than surplus commodities *no*
   (b) Medical inspection by nurse? *by teacher*
      By doctor? *no*
   (c) No. individuals inspected? *21*
   (d) No. individuals having defects? *one*
   (e) No. individuals having defects remedied? *none*
   (f) How many times was your school-room floor scrubbed this term? *once*

E. Is your school standardized for aid? *yes*

ENROLLMENT													TOTALS			GRADUATION						
GRADES	1	2	3	4	5	6	7	8	9	10	11	12	Boys	Girls	All	From Grades	12	Boys	Girls	Totals	All	
Farm boys	1	2		2			3							9				8					
Farm girls	2	1	3	1											12								
City boys	4														21								
City girls																							

b. No. days school was taught (all days for which pay will be received) - *160*
c. Aggregate days of teaching - *3360*
d. Aggregate attendance - *3006*
e. *Aggregate absence - *38*
f. **Aggregate non-membership - *36*
g. Average daily attendance (d ÷ b) - *18 t*
h. Per cent of attendance d ÷ (d + e) - *98 %*
   Verification: See that d plus e plus f equals, c. Also that a times b equals c.

1. No. visits of county superintendent - *two*
2. No. visits of deputy superintendent - *none*
3. No. visits of school officers - *two*
4. No. other visits - *ten*

1. No. books in library (not including text-books) - *twenty*
2. No. books per pupil per grade in library - *five*
3. No. books purchased this year - *none*
4. No. loaned this year - *none*

No. months school was taught, including all legal holidays and other days for which pay will be received - *eight*
No. of actual days of teaching (exclude holidays) - *149*
Salary of teacher per month - *$70.00*
Grades taught - *7*
No. classes taught per day - *25*

Is there a U. S. flag in your school? *yes*
Do you use it as required by law? - *yes*

*"Absence" means illegal non-attendance.
**"Non-membership" means legal non-attendance.

Daily Program and Classification
1942

Time	Min	Activity	Grade	Grade in exams when term completed	Promoted
9:00	10	Opening Ex	All	7	Exam
9:10	15	Reading	P.-1-2	4	to 5th on trial
9:25	15	Reading	3-4	5	to 6th
9:40	15	Reading	5	3	to 4th
9:55	20	Grammar	7-8	7	Exam
10:15	15	Numbers	P.-1-2-3	1	to 2nd
10:30	15	Supervised Play	All	7	Exam
10:45	36	Arithmetic	4-5-7-8	4	to 5th
11:#5	20	Spelling word drill	2-3-4-5-7-8	2	to 3rd
11:35	10	Pen & Art	P-1-2-3-4	P	to 1st
11:45	15	Clean up period	All	5	to 6th on trial
12:00	60	Lunch	All	P	to 1st
1:00	10	Checking Assignment	All	2	to 3rd
1:10	10	Reading - Language	P.-1-2	3	to 4th
1:20	10	Languages Geography	3-4	1	to 2nd
1:30	20	Geography	7	3	to 4th
1:50	10	Health & History	4-5	8	Exam
2:00	15	History	7	5	to 6th
2:15	15	History	8	Graduated in Dec. 1941	
2:30	15	Supervised Play	All	1	to 2nd
2:45	10	Reading	P.-1	8	Exam
2:55	10	word drill-phonics Reading	2-3-4		
3:05	10	Language - Reading	5		
3:15	20	Citizenship	8		
3:35	15	Agric & Health	7		
3:50	10	Literature - Reading	8		

School Year 1961-62

a. ENROLLMENT

GRADES	1	2	3	4	5	6	7	8	9	10	11	12	TOTALS Boys	TOTALS Girls	TOTALS All
Number Boys	1	1	1	1		2	2	2					4		
Number Girls	1	1	3	2	1	4	1	2						10	
Total by Grades															14

GRADUATION

From Grades	8	12	Totals Boys	Totals Girls	Totals All
	2			2	2

b. No. days school was taught (include all legal school holidays) - - - - - - *180*
c. Aggregate days of teaching - - - - *2520*
d. Aggregate attendance - - - - - *2490*
e. *Aggregate absence - - - - - - *30*
f. **Aggregate membership - - - - *2520*
g. Average daily attendance (d÷b) - - *13.83*
h. Average daily membership (f÷b) - - *14*
i. Per cent of attendance d÷(d+e) - - *98.80*
Verification: See that d plus e equals f.
Also that a times b equals c.

1. No. visits of county superintendent - - *2*
2. No. visits of deputy superintendent - - *0*
3. No. visits of school officers - - - - *4*
4. No. other visits - - - - - - - *10*

1. No. books in library (not including textbooks) - - - - - - - - - *113*
2. No. books per pupil per grade in library - *8*
3. No. books purchased this year - - - *15*
4. No. books loaned this year - - - - *20*

No. days school was taught. (include all legal school holidays) - - - - - - - *180*
No. of actual days of teaching (exclude legal school holidays) - - - - - - - *177*
Salary of teacher per month - - - - *$400*
Grades taught - - - - - - - *8*
No. classes taught per day - - - - -

Is there a U. S. flag in your school? - - *yes*
Do you use it as required by law? - - - *yes*

* "Absence" means non-attendance.
** "Membership" means days on rolls.

TEACHER'S REPORT

School No. *4*
of *Krassna* School District No. *39*
County of *Emmons*, State of North Dakota.

To County Superintendent of Schools:
I hereby submit my report for the term beginning *Sept. 4*, 19 *61*, and ending *May 18, 24*, 19 *62*
Mrs. Victoria Voller Teacher
Dated at, 19 *62*

Duplicate sent to clerk *5-28-*, 19 *62*
Report received *5-24-*, 19 *62*
Alvin M. Tarlovnik County Supt.

GENERAL STATEMENT

A. Teacher's Training and Experience:
  1. No. years completed above H. S. *1½ yrs.*
     Where *Ellendale* When
     Graduate Normal School
     Where When
     Graduate College or University
     Where When
  2. No. years experience *7*
     In N. D. *7* Outside State *0*
  3. Number and kind of Certificate *H 3005*
  4. Are you a member of N. D. E. A.? *no*
  5. Are you a member of the N. E. A.? *yes*
  6. New to State (From Outside)? *no*
  7. N. D. Teacher (1st Yr. in State)
  8. Taught in State Before *yes*
B. School Property:
  Repairs and supplies needed

C. Community Center Activities:
  1. Have you in your school district:
     (a) A Parent–Teacher Organization? *no*
     (b) A Boys' and Girls' Club? *yes*
     (c) Young Citizen's League Organization? *yes*
     (d) No. of Y. C. L. members? *14*
  2. How many school entertainments (not held in school hours)? *none*

D. Health Conservation:
  Have you in your school:
     (a) School Lunch Program? *no*
       (1) Reimbursed
       (2) Not Reimbursed
     (b) Medical inspection by nurse? *no*
       By doctor? *no*
     (c) No. individuals inspected?
     (d) No. individuals having defects?
     (e) No. individuals having defects remedied?

Daily Program and Classification
1962

Time	Subject	Grades
9:00	Opening Ex.	all
9:10	Reading	1-6
	Classics M W F	7-8
	Literature T T	7-8
	Grammar	7-8
10:30	Supervised Play	all
10:45	Arithmetic	all
	Spelling & Penmanship	all
12:00	Lunch	
12:30	Phonics	1-3
	English	4-6
	History M W F	7-8
	Geography M W F	4-8
	History T T	4-6
	N. Dak. History F	8
2:15	Supervised Play	all
2:30	Health T T Science M W	1-6
	Agriculture M W	7
	Art or Y C L F	all
3:30	Dismiss	

Angie Ibarra

Selected School Laws of North Dakota

§ 89. ONLY ENGLISH LANGUAGE TO BE TAUGHT.] All reports and records of school officers, and proceedings of all school meetings shall be kept in the English language, and if any money belonging to any district shall be expended in supporting a school in which the English language shall not be taught exclusively, the county superintendent, or any tax payer of the school corporation may, in civil action in the name of the corporation, recover for the corporation all such money from the officer or officers so expending it or ordering or voting for its expenditure.

HOUSE CONCURRENT RESOLUTION "E-1"
(Schmalenberger)

EMPHASIS IN SCHOOLS ON PENMAMSHIP AND SPELLING

A concurrent resolution directing greater emphasis in our schools be placed on the art of penmanship and the rudiments of spelling.

WHEREAS, communication by handwritten means is still the most prevalent method; and

WHEREAS, the art of penmanship, and the rudiments of spelling are no longer properly emphasized in our primary schools, high school nor in our teachers' colleges; and

WHEREAS, the art of writing legibly and accurately can only be learned and improved by reinstating and emphasizing teaching of penmanship and spelling by rote and by emphasizing its importance in society to students and teachers

WHEREAS, some of the most intelligent thoughts are o   lost or uncommunicated because of illegible handwriting today; and

WHEREAS, business men and others are observing increasing difficulty with the inability of their employees to spell properly;

Now, Therefore, Be It Resolved By The House Of Representatives Of The State Of North Dakota, The Senate Concurring Therein:

That the superintendent of public instruction, the board of public school, the board of higher education, the president of the various teachers colleges, and the principals of each elementary and secondary public school in this state, are hereby directed to place greater emphasis on instruction of students in the art of penmanship and the rules of spelling, so that our future adults will not be handicapped by inadequacy in these essential fields.

Be It Further Resolved, that copies of this resolution shall be sent by the secretary of state to the superintendent of public instruction, each member of the board of higher education, each member of the board of public school education. The superintendent of public instruction will mimeograph copies for principals of schools and presidents of each teachers college.

Filed March 8, 1957.

HOUSE CONCURRENT RESOLUTION "J"
(Hofstrand and Tollefson)
L.R.C. SCHOOL STUDY

Concurrent resolution directing the legislative research committee to study the organization, adminstration and financing of special education public schools, and schools of higher learning.

WHEREAS, the citizens and legislative assembly of the state of North Dakota have always considered the education of its citizens as one of its most important governmental duties and have made great efforts to constantly improve its system of public schools; and

WHEREAS, in spite of such efforts the schools of this state are still faced with a shortage of qualified teachers and inadequate curriculum and physical facilities; and

WHEREAS, in the agricultural state of North Dakota, of 360 high schools only 50 offer vocational agriculture and 100 offer home economics courses; and

WHEREAS, North Dakota financial problems in the field of public education are more difficult than those of many other states because of North Dakota's large area coupled with a small population with an inadequate financial structure and tax base which results in high per pupil costs of education; and

WHEREAS, because of limitations imposed by meager tax resources in North Dakota and statutory limitations imposed by an outmoded statutory structure governing school districts, further substantial progress in improving special elementary, secondary and junior college and higher education is extremely difficult;

Now, Therefore, Be It Resolved By The House Of Representatives Of The State Of North Dakota, The Senate Concurring Therein:

That the legislative research committee is authorized and directed to study and consider the organization, administration, financial resources and requirements, statutory limitations, obsolete or unworkable laws, and other matters affecting special elementary, secondary and junior college and higher education in North Dakota with a view of improving education in this state, together with a study of the existing program of vocational agriculture and vocational home economics and expansion of such programs into high schools of this state which are not presently participating therein, and providing for the greatest possible economy and efficiency. It shall specifically consider the feasibility of rearranging or reorganizing the school districts in North Dakota in keeping with the needs of today and the future in terms of trade areas, popualtion centers, natural barriers, financial resources and equality of tax contribution, and shall report its appraisals to the Thirty-sixth Legislative Assembly in the forms of bills, resolutions, proposed constitutional amendments, or otherwise as it may deem necessary.

Filed March 8, 1957.

Selected School Laws of North Dakota
page II

15-2507. School library: Appropriations; Use of; Penalties for misuse of books. For the purpose of acquiring a school library for each school in the district, the school board shall expend for each such school the following amounts:

1. Not less than twenty-five dollars each year until the library contains two hundred books;
2. Not less than ten dollars each year after the library contains two hundred books and until it contains three hundred books;
3. After the library contains three hundred books, the board shall not be required to purchase additional books to increase such number, but it shall keep the books in good condition and shall replace annually as many books as shall have become lost, destroyed, or obsolete.

Books purchased under this section shall be selected by the board and the teacher from any list of books authorized by the superintendent of public instruction and furnished by him to the county superintendent of schools. All such books shall be bound in cloth or in an equally durable material. Whenever school is in session and at all other practicable times, the library shall be kept in the schoolhouse, and no books shall be loaned from such library to any person who is not a resident of the school district. The board may impose and collect penalties for injuries done to books by the act, negligence, or permission of any person who takes or has possession thereof, and may exchange temporarily any part or all of any library in the district with any other district or person, but each district shall recall its books before the close of the school term. The board may accept donations of books for the library, but it shall exclude from the library all books unsuited to the cultivation of good character and good morals and manners. No sectarian publications devoted to the discussion of sectarian differences and creeds shall be admitted to the library.

Source: S. L. 1955, c.135.

15-2508. Teachers: Employment; Discharge; Qualifications; Written contract. The school board shall employ the teachers of the district and may dismiss a teacher at any time for plain violation of contract, gross immorality, or flagrant neglect of duty. No person related by blood or marriage to any member of the board shall be hired as a teacher without the unanimous consent of the board. No person shall be permitted to teach in any public school who is not the holder of a teacher's certificate or a permit to teach, valid in the county or district in which the school is situated. Every contract for the employment of a teacher shall be in writing, and shall be executed before the teacher begins to teach in such school, and each such contract shall provide that in the event of the discontinuance of a school term for lack of attendance as provided in this chapter, no compensation shall be paid to the teacher from the date of such discontinuance. No teacher holding a valid first grade elementary certificate shall receive less than nine hundred dollars per school term, a teacher holding a second grade professional certificate, shall not receive less than ten hundred eighty dollars per school term, and a teacher holding a first grade professional certificate shall not receive less than thirteen hundred fifty dollars, but this section shall not require teachers holding certificates of the same grade to receive the same salaries.

Source: S. L. 1947, c.142, s.1.

15-2604. Organization of school on petition of parents; Lease of rooms; Election; When purchase necessary. When a petition signed by persons charged with the support and having the custody and care of nine or more children of compulsory school age, all of whom reside not less than two and one-half miles by the usual route of travel from the nearest school, is presented to the school board of a common school district asking for the organization of a school for such children, the board shall organize a school and employ a teacher therefor if a suitable room for the school can be acquired by lease at some proper location not more than two and one-half miles distant from the residence of any of such children. The board shall not acquire any premises by lease for a longer period than one school year, and schools shall not be conducted in leased quarters for more than one school year unless there remain in the territory, within two and one-half miles of said school, nine or more children of compulsory school age, all of whom reside more than two and one-half miles from any other existing school in the district, in which case, the lease may be continued from year to year so long as such conditions exist. If no suitable room for the school can be leased or rented, the board shall call a meeting of the voters of the district for the purpose of selecting a site and purchasing or building a schoolhouse. If no site is selected at the meeting, or if the electors do not authorize the erection or purchase of a schoolhouse for such school, the board shall select and purchase a school site and purchase, erect, or move a schoolhouse thereon at a cost of not more than two thousand five hundred dollars for such schoolhouse and the furniture thereof. The provisions of this section shall not apply in cases where schools have been consolidated.

Source: S. L. 1931, c.248, s.1.

CHAPTER 15-38
TEACHERS' DUTIES

15-3801. Superintendent of city and village schools; Powers and duties.
The superintendent of schools, in districts where a superintendent is employed, shall supervise the administration of the courses of study, visit schools, examine classes, and have general supervision of the professional work of the schools, including the holding of teachers' meetings and the classification of teachers, all of which shall be subject to the final authority of the school board or board of education. From time to time, he shall make reports to the board embodying recommendations relative to the employment of teachers and janitors, the adoption of text books, changes in the courses of study, enforcement of discipline, and school matters in general. He shall make such other reports and perform such other duties as the board may direct and delegate.

Source: C. L. 1913, s.1378.

15-3802. Opening and closing of schools; Notice. Each teacher, on beginning a term of school, shall give written notice to the county superintendent of schools of the time and place of opening the school and the time when it probably will close. If the school is to be suspended for one week or more in the term, the teacher shall notify the county superintendent of such suspension.

Source: C. L. 1913, s.1379.

15-3803. Teacher's register: Contents; Report. Each teacher shall keep a school register and at the close of each term shall make a report stating the number of visits of the county superintendent of schools and such other items as may be required by the county superintendent. The report shall be made in duplicate, and both copies shall be sent to the county superintendent. If he finds the report correct, he shall send one copy immediately to the clerk of the school district, or to the secretary of the board of education, as the case may be. No teacher shall be paid any salary for the last month of a term until the report has been approved by the county superintendent and filed with the clerk.

Source: C. L. 1913, s.1381.

15-3804. School holidays defined; Schools to be taught; Exercises.
Every day which is designated by the laws of this state as a legal holiday also shall be a school holiday, but unless the day shall fall upon a Saturday or Sunday, schools shall be in session as usual on the following holidays:

1. February twelfth, Lincoln's Birthday;
2. February twenty-second, Washington's Birthday;
3. The first Monday in September, Labor Day;
4. October twelfth, Discovery Day;
5. November eleventh, Armistice Day; and
6. Every day upon which an election is held throughout the state.

On each of the days herein specified, at least one hour shall be devoted to patriotic exercises consistent with the day. School shall not be held on Armistice Day in coumunities in which community celebrations are held on that day, nor on election days in districts in which the schoolhouses are used for polling places, nor on any legal holiday not specified in this section. Each holiday upon whic the schools are closed under this section, if it falls upon a day which otherwis would be a school day, shall be counted as a school day, and the teachers sha be paid therefor.

Source: 1925 Supp., s.1382.

15-3805. Temperance Day; Duty of school officers and teachers. The third Friday in January of each year shall be set apart and designated as Temperance Day. In every public school in the state, not less than one hour of the school day shall be set apart for instruction and appropriate exercises, and the school shall continue its regular work during the remainder of the day. All state, county, city, and school district officers, and all public school teachers, shall carry out the provisions of this section.

Source: 1925 Supp., s.7299a.

15-3806. Teachers to be excused to vote. If necessary, any teacher who cannot use an absent voter's ballot shall be excused from school, without loss of pay, on any day on which an election is held throughout the state, to permit him to go to his voting precinct to vote.

Source: 1925 Supp., s.1382.

15-3807. Required subjects in the public school. The following subjects shall be taught in the public schools to pupils who are sufficiently advanced to pursue the same: spelling, reading, writing, arithmetic, language, English grammer, geography, United States history, civil government, nature study, and elements of agriculture. Physiology and hygiene also shall be taught, and in teaching such subject, the teacher shall:

1. Give special and thorough instruction concerning the nature of alcoholic drinks and narcotics and their effect upon the human system;
2. Give simple lessons in the nature, treatment, and prevention of tuberculosis and other contagious and infectious diseases;
3. Give, to all pupils below the high school and above the third year of school work, not less than four lessons in hygiene each week for ten weeks of each school year from text books adapted to the grade of the pupils;
4. Give, to all pupils in the three lowest primary school years, not less than three oral lessons on hygiene each week for ten weeks of each school year, using text books adapted to the grade of the pupils as guides or standards for such instruction.

Source: C. L. 1913, s.1383.

15-3808. Study of constitution of the United States. In all public and private schools in the state, regular courses of instruction in the constitution of the United States shall be given, beginning not later than the opening of the eighth grade and continuing in the high school, to an extent to be determined by the superintendent of public instruction.

Source: S. L. 1929, c.210, ss.1,2.

15-3809. Physical education to be taught in all schools. Physical education shall be taught as a regular subject to all pupils in all departments of the public schools and in all educational institutions supported wholly or in part by money from the state. All school boards and boards of education and boards of educational institutions receiving money from the state shall make provision for daily instruction in all the schools and institutions under their respective jurisdictions and shall adopt such methods as will adapt progressive physical exercises to the development, health, and discipline of the pupils in the various grades and classes of such schools and institutions.

Source: C. L. 1913, s.1390.

15-3810. Moral instruction. Moral instruction tending to impress upon the minds of pupils the importance of truthfulness, temperance, purity, public spirit, patriotism, international peace, respect for honest labor, obedience to parents, and deference to old age, shall be given by each teacher in the public schools.

Source: C. L. 1913, s.1389.

15-3811. Teaching humane treatment of animals. Oral instruction in the humane treatment of animals shall be given in each public school.

Source: C. L. 1913, s.1384.

15-3812. Reading of Bible optional. The Bible shall not be deemed a sectarian book. At the option of the teacher, it may be read in school for not to exceed ten minutes daily, but no sectarian comment shall be made thereon. No pupil shall be required to read it or to be present in the schoolroom during the reading thereof contrary to the wishes of his parents or guardians or other person having him in charge.

Sourse: C. L. 1913, s.1388.

15-3813. Suspension of pupils; Cause; Notice. A teacher may suspend any pupil from school for not more than five days for insubordination, habitual disobedience, or disorderly conduct. In each case, the teacher shall give immediate notice of the suspension, and the reason therefor, to the parent or guardian of the pupil and to a member of the school board or board of education.

Source: 1925 Supp., s.1386.

15-3814. Assignment of studies to pupils: Classification of pupils. The teacher, or the principal or local superintendent in graded schools under the charge of a principal or local superintendent, shall assign to each pupil, in accordance with the provisions of this chapter, such studies as he is qualified to pursue and shall place such pupil in the proper grade or class in the school. If any parent or guardian in a common school district shall be dissatisfied with such assignment or classification, the matter shall be referred to and decided by the county superintendent of schools when the school is under his supervision.

Source: C. L. 1913, s.1387.

15-3815. Duty to attend teachers' institutes and training schools; Notice; Penalty for failure to attend. When a teachers' institute or teachers' training school is appointed to be held in or for any county, the county superintendent of schools shall give written or printed notice thereof and of the time when and the place where the same will be held to each teacher in the public schools of the county, and, as far as possible, to others not then engaged in teaching who are holders of teachers' certificates. The notice shall be given at least ten days before the opening of the institute or teachers' training school. Each teacher who receives the notice, and who is engaged in teaching a term of school during the time when the teachers' institute or training school is in session, shall close the school and attend the institute or training school, and shall be paid the regular salary as teacher by the board of the school district for the time during which he is in attendance as certified by the county superintendent of schools. No teacher shall receive pay for such attendance unless he has attended four days, nor shall any teacher receive pay for more than five days of attendance. The county superintendent of schools may revoke the certificate of any teacher in the county for inexcusable neglect or refusal, after due notice, to attend a teachers' institute or teachers' training school held for the county. The provisions of this section shall not apply to high school teachers, nor to teachers in cities organized for school purposes under a special law or as independent districts under the provisions of this title.

Source: 1925 Supp.. s.1385.

CHAPTER 15-47
GENERAL PROVISIONS

15-4701. Schools free and accessible; School ages. The public schools of the state shall be equally free, open, and accessible at all times to all children between the ages of six and twenty-one except that children who do not arrive at the age of six years by midnight, December thirty-first, shall not start school until the beginning of the following school year.

Source: S. L. 1955, c.145.

15-4702. State institutions of higher education are part of free public school system. The university and the school of mines at Grand Forks, the agricultural college at Fargo, the state normal schools at Valley City, Mayville, Minot, and Dickinson, and school for the deaf and dumb at Devils Lake, the school of forestry at Bottineau, the school of science at Wahpeton, the normal and industrial school at Ellendale, and all other schools established by law and maintained by taxation constitute the system of free public schools of the state.

Source: 1925 Supp., s.1415.

15-4703. English language to be used in schools. All reports and records of school officers and proceedings of school meetings shall be in the English language. If any money belonging to a school district shall be expended in supporting a school in which the English language is not the medium of instruction exclusively, the county superintendent of schools or any taxpayer of the district, in a civil action in the name of the district, may recover for the district all such money from the officer expending it or ordering or voting for its expenditure.

Source: C. L. 1913, s.1199.

15-4704. School year, month, and week defined. The school year shall begin on the first day of July and shall close on the thirtieth day of June of the following year. A school month shall consist of twenty days, and a school week shall consist of five days.

Source: 1925 Supp., s.1382.

15-4705. Qualifications of school electors and officers. Any person who is a qualified elector under the general laws of the state is qualified to vote at the election of school officers in any school district of the state in which he is a resident, and is eligible to the office of school director, district treasurer, school district clerk, or member of the board of education, or may be appointed as a judge or clerk of election.

Source: C. L. 1913, s.1153.

15-4710. Ten commandments to be displayed in classrooms. The school board or board of education of every school district, and the president of every institution of higher education in the state which is supported by appropriations or by tax levies, shall cause a placard containing the ten commandments of the Christian religion to be displayed in a conspicuous place in every schoolroom, classroom, or other place where classes convene for instruction. The superintendent of public instruction may cause such placards to be printed and may charge an amount therefor that will cover the cost of printing and distribution.

Source: S. L. 1927, c.247, ss. 1,2.

15-4711. United States flag to be displayed. The school board or board of education of every school district shall purchase, at the expense of the district, one or more flags of the United States. Such flag shall be displayed in seasonable weather on each schoolhouse or upon a flagstaff on the school grounds of each school during the school hours of each day's session of school.

Source: C. L. 1913, s.1400.

15-4712. Legislation. Legislation proposed or advocated by or in behalf of any person, institution, or educational interest affecting education, and any proposed amendments to the school laws, shall be submitted whenever possible, on or before November fifteenth preceding the regular session of the legislative assembly, to the state board of higher education if the proposals relate to any of the institutions governed by the board, or, when not relating to any such institutions, to the superintendent of public instruction. The proposed legislation, together with any comments thereon made by the state board of higher education or the superintendent of public instruction, shall be published and copies shall be presented to the members of the legislative assembly.

Source: C. L. 1913, s.1742.

Celebrations

What You'll See
at the
Golden Jubilee Celebration
In Linton
Friday-Saturday, Oct. 5-6

The Three Larconians
(Two Acts Daily)

A mixture of Equilibrism, Buffoonery and Novel Stunts. All numbers are fast, funny and flashy, with tumbling, acrobatic and contortion added for good measure.

You'll like this trio of comedians

Dashington's Animals
Dogs and Cats

Celebration

Praise and celebrate your life,
   and there will be more to Celebrate.

The Krassna settlers had many celebrations. The G/Rs were
an intense group. They worked hard, played hard, and prayed a lot.
They attended a lot of dances either in Strasburg, or at barn dances
on neighboring farms. The instrument and dance of choice were the
accordion and the polka.

Birthdays were not often celebrated, instead namesdays were
celebrated, a Catholic tradition. As one of the priests would say,
"Every dog has a Birthday." On the day of a Saint's Feast Day,
whoever had the same name as that saint would have a big celebration
with lots of food and many visitors. When it was the church feast day,
for whatever saint or event the church was named after, there would be
an even bigger celebration. All the relatives from near and far would
come to the church and after church visit at your home. There would
be an abundance of food and merriment.

Christmas was mostly a religious holiday. It was such a beautiful
event. Riding through the drifting snow, we would go to midnight
mass. The church would be lit up with candles. The choir singing
"Silent Night" in German was particularly lovely, as was the smell of
incense. The candles and the mass spoken in Latin seemed very exotic.
   The schools would have a Christmas celebration that was a big
social event. Teachers had it written into their contracts that they
would have a play day for Christmas, and other times too. All the
students would look forward to participating in the Christmas Play.
   When I was five I was asked to say a poem in front of the
audience. It was probably quite comical to hear me say it with my
thick German accent.

Exchanging presents was not common. Usually, for Christmas, your godparents would give you a brown paper bag containing fruits and nuts. Fruits were a treat as they were not readily available out on the prairie.

Occasionally we had a Christmas tree in our home, which my dad would get across the river in Fort Yates. Trees were a treasured commodity so they were not usually cut down for a celebration. My older brother dressed up as Santa Claus, even though we all knew that he was Santa.

My most memorable Christmas was when I asked for a paint set. There must have been a crop failure that year and my parents could not afford very much, so instead I got a pencil and tablet for my Christmas present. I remember my mother telling me that they just could not get the paint set for me. I think she felt worse than I did. I will always remember that Christmas because I always felt they gave me everything they could. I asked my mother about Santa Claus, I knew she would tell me the truth. I don't remember her explanation but to this day I still believe in Santa Claus. After all Santa Claus is the spirit of giving.

Easter was another religious holiday and there were special events leading up to it. Before the 40 days of Lent started there would be a big celebration called *Fastnacht* (Fast night). There would be barn dances, or dances at Strasburg at the Blue Room. There was a special food called pig ears. It was similar to a donut except it was a triangle. It was deep fried and sprinkled with powdered sugar. One explanation that I heard is that you needed to give up sugar and oil for Lent, so you used up all those ingredients to make the pigs ears.

On Palm Sunday palms were given out at church. A G/R Catholic tradition was to braid the palms with four palms overlapping. These were later placed behind a religious picture or crucifix. They were mostly a decorative item. On Holy Thursday people would bake bread, cookies, and other foods, and bring them to church for a special blessing.

On Easter we would have colored eggs placed in holes dug out in the yard .We colored them with a dye to which vinegar had been added. I can still remember the smell of the vinegar. One time on Good Friday I was digging a hole in preparation to putting in my Easter eggs that the Easter bunny was probably going to bring me. My mother told me I should not be digging holes on Good Friday as that was the day

Jesus died and it would be like trying to dig Him up.

The 4th of July was a really big celebration that required dress-up clothes. Many of the farmers brought their families to Strasburg for the big celebration. We would go to Strasburg and visit our aunt and uncle. They had a refrigerator which had metal ice cube trays. They had ice cubes made out of nectar, which is now called KoolAid and was similar to popsicles. It was so delicious to put it on your tongue and have it melt in your mouth. I think cherry was the only flavor available. This was quite a novelty as no one in Krassna owned a refrigerator, since there was no electricity. They also did not have an ice box, as early refrigerators were called, because we did not have a person delivering ice.

Another 4th of July event would be to go to the Keller Hardware store and buy rolls of caps and other fireworks. I would get caps and pound them with a rock to make them pop. I can almost still smell the gun powder. After a big parade, several politicians would give speeches at the Gazebo located in the center of town. We had lots of fun and games. Later our parents would go to a dance. It was too far to drive home to Krassna and back and we did not have baby sitters, so sometimes we children attended the dances as well.

Halloween was a religious holiday called "All Saints Day," followed by All Souls Day when you would pray for the dead, especially for any relatives that had recently died. Sometimes an activity we played in school was bobbing for apples. This game was played by filling a large tub to the top with water and an apple for each player, smaller apples were best for this game because they are easier to bite into. The players took turns trying to retrieve an apple using only their mouth and placing their heads in the tub. This is quite difficult, since the apples bob around as students tried to bite into them. Players who were able to retrieve an apple were rewarded with a prize. Thanksgiving was celebrated with a lot of food and visitors. Sometimes goose rather than turkey was on the menu.

Valentine's Day was a celebration at school with homemade valentines. The teacher decorated a box and placed it on her desk for students to drop in the Valentines.

Weddings were big events which were usually celebrated either before planting or after the harvest. Weddings took place in the morning on Mondays or Tuesdays rather than on the weekend. Family members would prepare the food for the weddings. I have never attended weddings in any other part of the country which had such an abundance of good food. There was even a special wedding kuchen (a custard fruit pie), a little different than regular kuchen, the German signature food.

Weddings were celebrated first at church and later at a dance most likely in Strasburg, at the Blue Room. At the entry way would be a person serving Red Eye made with Everclear, alcohol flavored with cherry juice and caramelized sugar as the guests arrived.

At the beginning of the wedding dance the accordionist would greet the bride and groom at the entrance and play while following them to the dance floor. The rest of the wedding party would follow. The bride would have the first dance with the groom, followed by the bride with her father. The groom and groom's mother then danced together before everyone began switching partners. Then the rest of the guests would join in. The danceing continued until dinner was served at noon.

Someone at the wedding would clatter a plate with a spoon and guests would put money in the plate for the musicians. After dinner people would dance again until supper which was another big feast. Sometime after supper the dance would be open to the public.

Since people traveled some distance, meaning several miles on country roads, they would probably stay overnight and continue the celebration the next day.

Most couples did not go on a honeymoon and more than likely lived with their parents on the farm until they were able to purchase their own. This changed considerably by the 1950s.

Summer threshing time was something to look forward to. We would have hired hands to help with the threshing and young ladies to help my mother prepare all the food needed to feed the crew. Sometimes I would go along to deliver food to the workers out in the field. Food was served to the workers before and after the noon meal.

We had large noon meals (dinner) with lots of pies, kuchen and other goodies as the threshing crew worked hard and had to be well fed to keep up their strength.

There was a rhythm to farm life. The weather seasons, the planting season, the harvest season, calving, butchering, feast days, weddings, school days and life was never boring.

Angie's brother Lawrence prepareing their horse for a celebration.

EMMONS COUNTY RECORD

Linton Theatre

Thursday, Friday, Saturday   April 25-26-27

MATINEE SATURDAY AT 2:00 P. M

BING CROSBY AND INGRID BERGMAN IN

"The Bells of St. Mary's"

Sunday, Monday, Tuesday   April 28-29-30

JOHN PAYNE, MAUREEN O'HARA, WILLIAM BENDIX IN

"SENTIMENTAL JOURNEY"

ALSO NEWS AND SHORTS

Wednesday and Thursday   May 1-2

HEDY LAMARR, ROBERT WALKER, JUNE ALLYSON IN

"HER HIGHNESS AND THE BELLBOY"

ALSO LATEST NEWS AND SHORTS

EMMONS COUNTY RECORD
OFFICIAL NEWSPAPER OF EMMONS COUNTY AND CITY OF LINTON

Strasburg Offers' Splendid Program
PARADE, RACES, FIREWORKS, BOXING FEATURE OF JULY 4 CELEBRATION

A splendid program of entertainment for all who go to Strasburg to celebrate on July 4 is promised by the businessmen of that town who yesterday completed the final arrangements for the big-time.

A street parade at 10:00 in the morning will start off the events of the day which will continue well into the late evening. A prominent speaker will address the crowd at 10:45. A lengthy program of sports events will follow at 11 o'clock. These include eight scheduled foot races for boys, girls, men and women. Cash prizes up to $1.50 will be given the winners for first, second, and third places.

There will be a balloon busting contest for boys for cash prizes. A Shetland pony race with cash awards of two dollars and one dollar for first and second place will bring the morning contest to a close. Every family entering a Shetland pony in the parade will be given $1 in cash.

In the afternoon there will be several novelty races including a bicycle race, pony potato race and a three-legged race for boys and young men for cash prizes. Clowns will entertain the kiddies and distribute free candy and peanuts.

Featured in the afternoon program are a baseball game between the old rivals Strasburg and Linton, a first-class boxing card at the North Side Pool Hall, and a grand display of daylight fireworks at the baseball grounds.

Headliners on the boxing card are Tony Braun, successful fighter from the west who will box Howard Bush, the best in the state, in a winner- take-all match. For the semi windup, Tuffy Masset, Bismarck, will meet Howard Ludgke of Aberdeen in a return grudge fight. There will also be nine rounds of preliminaries.

The Strasburg Firemen's Band will give a concert on the street at 7 PM. Plenty of concession stands will be provided serving lunches, drinks and confections to the public. The town's new 50 x 100 dance hall has just been completed where dancing can be enjoyed continuously during the afternoon and evening.

EMMONS COUNTY RECORD

9-21-1933

Krassna

By Harry Nagel

While I'm over here this week hauling corn fodder, might as well call the items "Krassna."

A birthday party was celebrated at the Joe Glass place Saturday evening, it being Mrs. (?) birthday. A delicious lunch was served at midnight and everybody had a great time.

Mr. and Mrs. Joe Nagel and, Mr. and Mrs. Ray Bickler, Mr. and Mrs. Ben Marquert, and Mr. and Mrs. Peter Zacher went to Minot on Wednesday, returning home Friday. They report a very interesting and sightseeing trip. They were among the many attending the free street entertainment in Linton on their way home.

Mr. and Mrs. Christ. Schaff and son Steve of Solen and the former's brother from Minnesota were visiting Rochus Nagel Thursday.

Mr. and Mrs. Mike Masseth and Mr. and Mrs. Rochus Nagel were Sunday afternoon visitors at the Max Nagel place.

Joe Glas went to Minneapolis Sunday morning to visit A.N. Drake who is sick in the hospital there.

Mr. and Mrs. Mike Nagel and Sebold and Isadore Nagel were visiting with Mr. and Mrs. Elias Nagel Jr. , Sunday.

Mr. and Mrs. Joe Huen were Sunday visitors at the Peter Fiest place.

Johnny Wagner and Harry Heidrich were seen going by here Sunday night for my home in Winona. The boys report a party at the Wendelin Schineider place. The evening was spent in dancing, etc.

Mr. and Mrs. Rochus Nagel went to Krassna Sunday night to visit Mr. and Mrs. Magnus. Wagner.

Miss Maggie Vetter was doing housework for Joe Nagel the past week.

Another good windstorm came up Monday night. It was blowing to beat---- but no rain this time. It rained a little Friday, soaking down fairly well.

Community

Angie's family in Krassna, North Dakota.
Rose, Ignatius, Iawrence, Johanna,
baby Angeline, and Peter

Community

To everything there is a season and a time to every purpose under the heaven: A time to be born and a time to die; a time to plant and a time to pluck up that which is planted.

(Eccl. 3:1-2)

Krassna was a vibrant community. Farm life was hard. The mantra might have been, work hard, play hard and pray. Most of the work revolved around farm life: planting, harvesting, milking and taking care of the animals. The change of seasons brought on many different types of duties.

During the winter months the men used their spare time to mend anything that was broken and needed fixing, especially machinery. If the machinery was not broken it needed oiling and other upkeep. The women kept busy making rag rugs, sewing clothes, making items out of flour sacks, cooking, baking, and taking care of the children.

The older children attended school. After school, when the children were not working, playing involved building snow houses and forts. My brothers would also go sledding on the hill by our farm with some of the neighbor children, using tires and other impromptu sleds.

One incident involving snow houses happened on a Saturday shortly after I started school. I wanted to show my little sister our school house with its water pail and dipper, and the desks. She was less adventuresome then me. I talked her into going to the school with me, which was about a mile away. On the way home she refused to cross a ditch filled with a lot of snow. I put boards that were lying nearby across the ditch, but she still refused to cross. Eventually, I got her to cross thus coming home later then planned. When we returned home we ran into my brother who informed me that my mother was really upset with me. Not knowing how to circumvent what might be punishment, we hid in the snow house that my brother had built earlier. Finally, it got very cold and we were hungry, so decided the punishment could not be worse than freezing and starving, so we went into the house. I asked my mother if she was upset with me and found out she did not even know we were gone.

Many hours would be spent indoors, due to the large amounts of snow and the extreme cold. The country roads were not always passable, so a horse and buggy would be used. Sometimes even then you could not get through, so isolation was a large part of winter.

My dad solved the isolation problem by using his entrepreneurial traits. He rigged up a phone with the neighbors, who lived on the other side of the hill. By using copper wires and a wooden wall phone, his creation was much like an intercom with two cans and a wire. Although, his was a little more sophisticated. This allowed my family and the neighboring family to communicate thus alleviating some of the isolation when traveling was not possible.

One type of entertainment for the family was listening to the radio, both for pleasure and the news. Many winter evenings would be spent with the family gathered around the radio listening to the news, particularly during elections and later during the war years.

One of the radio programs women listened too was: *Ma Perkins*, —sometimes called *Oxydol's Own Ma Perkins*, a radio soap opera. The program was heard from 1933 to 1960.

Known as "America's mother of the air," Ma Perkins was a gentle trusting widow with a big heart and a great love of humanity. She owned and operated a lumber yard in the small southern town of Rushville Center. The plot consisted of her interaction with the locals and the ongoing predicaments of her three children; Every, Fay, and John. Many crises intermingled with the shedding of tears, added to the drama. With her down to earth philosophy she offered advice to those who felt they needed it, or wanted to hear another point of view.

Lux Soap also had a popular radio series featuring *The Life and Love of Dr. Susan*. Dr. Susan returns to Valleydale to help her father-in-law with his medical practice, after her husband disappears while on a jungle expedition.

For the men the genre were cowboy programs such as the *Lone Ranger* with his white horse Silver and *Gene Autry* and his horse Champion, starting in 1933. The opening music alone was worth listening too. I listened to the programs also, thus spurring me on to my dream career of becoming a cowgirl.

Most people had a radio. Listening to it however, might be

limited, as it required huge batteries which were somewhat expensive.
Periodically, the tubes also went bad and had to be replaced. Turning
on the right station required skilled techniques, as the tuning did not
always work and you would be exposed to a lot of crackling noise.
The newscasters were particularly dramatic, adding to the appeal of
listening to the radio.

Angie and her family ready to drive to town.

In the spring and summer there were occasional trips to Strasburg
or some of the surrounding communities. Sometimes we attended fairs
in other communities. I remember going to Pollock to a fair. I thought
the hamburgers were the greatest and I also got a Kewpie doll which I
still have.

We also attended events in Strasburg. I remember attending a
magic show, which I really enjoyed. Vacations were not something
that was done. Probably because farming required doing daily chores.
I don't recall that we ever went to Bismarck, the closest big city, as a
family. Occasionally there were visits to a relative who might be in the
hospital in Bismarck, but only my parents would go.

Going to Linton was a big event, as they had a Penney's store
which was a major attraction. It contained dolls and toys and clothing,
which were fun to look at, even if not purchased. If anything was
purchased, an elaborate system sent the money to a cashier somewhere
upstairs. It consisted of a little round, metal box where the money
was placed and then sent on a long wire contraption, which in my
childhood mind was fun to watch.

Walking around Linton was also an adventure. There would
be Indians in teepees, some containing sewing machines which the

Indians used. This was very strange to my childhood eyes. Sometimes when I walked down the street with my mother people would stop us to ask if they could adopt me because our whole family, except for my younger sister, had bright red hair. We were probably the only people with red hair in Krassna. Both my parents had black hair. I had an outgoing personality and was willing to be adopted, much to my mother's umbrage, as I thought that would be a whole new adventure.

Strasburg was interesting as well; we would go to the Blue Room which was a bar, sometimes a dance hall, a movie theater or a roller skating rink. These were the social meeting places for the residents and the surrounding community. They also sold ice cream cones. My sister and I would each get a nickel to buy a cone. One time when I was in Strasburg a little Dutch boy came up to me and wanted to know what my name was. I understood what he was asking, but was unable to respond in English. I remember he got very mad at me. Another exciting thrill was to look into the barber shop window on main street and watch men get a shave and/or a haircut.

Other adventures in diversity were when the Gypsies occasionally came around. We were told they would steal children, but I don't think any were ever taken. However, they did take many other things. They even used to milk cows out in the pasture and steal the milk. I suppose they were hungry and didn't have any food. When they came to town everyone locked their doors. One person told me she had a prized doll; the only one she had. Later after the Gypsies came through it was gone.

We had a big hill not far from our house. That part of North Dakota had many flat hills but this one was round and pointed. We were not supposed to go up there, mostly because of the rattle snakes. My brother and I did go up there sometimes. He showed me several Indian artifacts. He told me one big rock, which was carved out in the middle was where the Indians took baths. He also showed me some arrowheads, which he found.

There were coyotes up in the hills and during mating season the howling sounds they made at night were blood-curdling and spine tingling. We were told that if we did not behave the wolves would get us, so of course we behaved. Life was sometimes happy, sometimes sad, but never dull. Thus the saga of life in the Krassna community continued without considerable change until after the war years.

Angie's father, Ignatius, on the roof of the barn he built. When the Reinbolds moved to this farm they lived in the original sod house built by the first Ingatius, his father.

Rose Ternes Silbernagel

Rose Ternes Silbernagel was born in 1921. She married Peter Silbernagel in 1943 at the Holy Trinity Catholic Church in Krassna, North Dakota. They farmed and also owned and operated Hillside grocery in Linton, North Dakota. They had fifteen children. Nine sons and six daughters, one was adopted.

Rose's priorities were God and family. She enjoyed reading, playing cards and cooking. She was involved in various organizations including Girl Scouts and Cub Scouts. Rose was chosen North Dakota Merit Mother in 1990-91. She will be remembered for her faith, generosity, humor and love of family and life.

Rose's godfather was her uncle, Lawrence Welk, who was born near Krassna. She was a very loving person, treating everyone as special. She died in 2010 at the age of 88. Rose was the author of most of the Krassna columns.

Lydia Ternes Roehrich

Lydia Ternes Roehrich, sister to Rose, was born in 1927. In 1948 she married Egidi Roehrich at Holy Trinity Catholic Church in Krassna, ND. They had 13 children. Eight girls and five boys. Egidi and Lydia farmed close to Krassna. They moved to Strasburg in 1979 where Egidi was mayor of Strasburg for several years.

Lydia resides in Strasburg and still loves playing cards, reading, cooking, and embroidering items for her family. She enjoys talking to her children on the phone or in person. Like her sister Rose, her priorities are God and family, faith generosity, humor and love of family and life. Lydia also authored some of the columns.

Harry Nagel

Harry Nagel periodically wrote articles for the Emmons County Record." He also occasionally authored some of the Krassna columns. Harry was born in 1914. In 1940 he married Philippina Schumacher. They had four children. He farmed in the Katzebauch area close to Krassna until 1943. Harry died in 1992 at the age of 78.

EMMONS COUNTY RECORD
OFFICIAL NEWSPAPER OF EMMONS COUNTY AND CITY OF LINTON

2-20-1936
KRASSNA
By Rose Ternes

Mrs. Dionyious Braun is on the sick list, but is recovering rapidly. Miss Isabel Braun, teacher of the Mattern school, visited at her home Wednesday. She is boarding at the Martin Roth place. Joe Biegler got stuck on his way to town. He had to shovel quite a ways, till his brother Pius came and pulled him out with the horses Jack Kramer got kicked by a horse last week.

Mrs. Max Tschosik went to Linton Saturday with the train. She wanted to get her set of false teeth. Our mail carrier is still bringing out the mail with his snow car., The weather surely is cold. Everybody is talking about it. One neighbor said that one morning it was so cold that when he started to milk the cows gave no milk, but little bits of ice.

Krassna School No. 1 had a Valentine party. They enjoyed themselves singing songs. The teacher told us the meaning of Valentines and read stories

---

3-15-1936
KRASSNA
By Rose Ternes

"Fazenacht" was celebrated at the Anton N. Ternes place Saturday night, Feb. 23. All had a good time in singing these beloved old time songs.

Miss Agatha Brickner was an overnight visitor at the Dionysious place Sunday night. Lydia, 9 year old daughter of Mr. and Mrs. Anton N. Ternes, was on the sick list the past week, but is fine now.

The namesday, Romanus, was celebrated at the Roy Ternes place Friday night, Feb. 28. J. Schwahn celebrated her 7th birthday Friday night. A few of her young friends gathered.

Mrs. Leopold Schwahn made her a nice birthday cake. Andrew Selzer is back home again after being in the hospital a long time with pneumonia.

Mr. and Mrs. Leopold Schwahn tipped the sled on the way to the Anton Ternes place Friday night. No one was hurt, however

99

EMMONS COUNTY RECORD

3-19-1936

KRASSNA
By Rose Ternes

Elenor Reinbold and Roy Wagner were married on Tuesday, Feb. 18. Their wedding dance was held the same evening at the A.J. Baumgartner hall. A wedding shower was given in their honor Thursday of the same week, also held at the Baumgartner hall at 7:30 p.m.

A big storm arose Monday and all the pupils of Krassna School No. 1 had to stay in school until almost dark when their parents came and took them home. The next day most of the pupils were absent.

Miss Agatha Brickner was an overnight guest at the Wendlin Kramer place Wednesday, Feb. 19. Mr. and Mrs. Balzar B. Mattern were visiting Wednesday and Thursday at the Wendlin Kramer place.

Erhard Braun the seven-year-old son of Mr. and Mrs. Dionyious Braun, had the measles this week and had to miss a few days of school. Theophila Braun was on the sick list Saturday and Sunday but is feeling fine now.

Joe Biegler was at his home Wednesday. He came with his truck although the roads were very bad. Leave it to Joe he'll pull through.

Saturday was George Washington's birthday, but school No. 1 celebrated it on Friday, Feb. 21. We sang a few patriotic songs and the teacher read us the "Life of Washington." Each grade had to sing a Washington song and the 5th grade did the best.

The class is as follows: Oscar A. Ternes, Selma Ternes, Philippine Kramer, Sybella Kramer, and Helen J. Tshosik.

Each pupil recited the poem of Washington, "A Boy's Privilege," by Freeman.

Miss Pauline Feist came home from Linton Saturday nite after working for her grandmother for about 2 months.

Romanus Brickner has been ill for a few days with a bad cold.

Mr. and Mrs. Anton N. Ternes were callers at Strasburg Sunday. They visited at Mrs. Anton Mattern's place; also at their folk's place, Louis Welk Sr.

Peter B. Biegler was in town Saturday. He had planned to get a load of coal, but they didn't have any in town. He brought out a 50-gallon barrel of kerosene for the Krassna store.

Mrs. Mary Tschosik is wearing her new set of false teeth. She looks dandy.

The Mr. and Mrs. And their two oldest sons were visiting at the John J. Tschosik place Sunday.

EMMONS COUNTY RECORD

3-26-1936
KRASSNA
By Rose Ternes

Anton Ternes, Mike D. Fiest and Mike J. Baumgartner took loads of grain to the Mrs. R. Schwab farm for Leopold Schwahn where they will make their home soon.

Quite a few farmers were transacting business in Linton last week Tuesday.

Eva Welk spent two days out in the country at the Anton Ternes place last week Thursday and Friday.

The namesday Joe was celebrate at the Joe Reinbold place Thursday. Friends and neighbors gathered.

John Tschosik was the first to be seen working in the field this year around the vicinity.

4-16-1936
KRASSNA
By Rose Ternes

Felix Mattern spent his Easter vacation at the Mike L. Welk home.

D. Brown and family were callers at Strasburg Sunday afternoon.

Mr. Tony Mattern and children and Mr. and Mrs. Ludwig Welk Sr. were out at the Mike Welk place Monday. They cleaned their car and afterwards Mrs. Welk served ice cream.

The writer is working at the Mike L. Welk place. She started work Monday.

All the farmers are busy as bees working out in the field, sowing wheat. Many young folks from this vicinity were in Strasburg Monday night. They had a good time at the dance.

4-19-1936
KRASSNA
By Rose Ternes

Krassna school No. 1 had their party Thursday. All were present and had a good time playing different games and eating ice cream.

All the farmers are preparing for spring work but it seems to all that the weather will never let them start.

Miss Mary M. Fischer, the Red Cross county nurse, examined all the pupils in Krassna school No. 1.

John Tschosik is the owner of a second hand Fordson tractor. He bought it last week and his son Adam is supposed to run it this spring.

John Baumgartner has been quite ill for a few weeks.

Mr. and Mrs. Steve B. Wagner were moving last week. They will make their home about four miles north of Strasburg.

Mr. and Mrs. John M. Ternes and Mr. and Mrs. Louis L. Welk and daughters are visiting at the Anton Ternes place Sunday night.

Joe Biegler will be home soon helping his dad and brother with spring work. A happy Easter and many greetings to my readers.

4-23-1936
KRASSNA
By Rose Ternes

Wendelin B. Biegler is working at home again.

Mary Young and old folks were visiting at the Anton N. Ternes place Sunday.

Miss Aurora Ternes was a caller in Strasburg Sunday.

Lydia Ternes visited at the Nick Ternes place Monday.

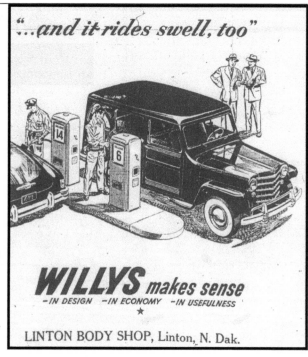

EMMONS COUNTY RECORD

5-21-1936
KRASSNA
By Rose Ternes

Miss Auroro Ternes and this writer spent a few days last week helping Mrs. Markus Franck cleaning house.

Mr. and Mrs. Adam Freiz of Flasher spent a few days in Strasburg and Krassna visiting friends and relatives

Mr. and Mrs. Nick N. Ternes and baby were at Solen last week on account of their mother's illness.

Mrs. R.H. and daughter were helping Mrs. Ben Biegler clean house Saturday.

Mrs. Anton Ternes celebrated her 36th birthday Monday.

5-26-1936
KRASSNA
By Rose Ternes

Nick Ternes is the proud owner of a Chevrolet car which he bought at Mandan.

The Mattern school where Isabel Braun is teaching had their picnic Wednesday, May 20. All had a good time. Miss Braun with her car and one of her pupils Edward J. Piest, with his dad's car took all the pupils to the big hill near the F. Braun place.

Mr. and Mrs. Johnny Welk of Ipswich were visiting friends and relatives at Strasburg Sunday and Monday.

Most of our housecleaning is done again.

Nick Ternes received a bad cut last week.

"Be careful so you won't be fooled by Johnny F. Braun."

EMMONS COUNTY RECORD

6-11-36

KRASSNA

By Rose Ternes

Mr. and Mrs. Ansel Sehn and daughters of Linton were visiting friends and relatives at Krassna Sunday.

Rev. Father Eichner announced Sunday that the children of this parish will receive their first Holy Communion on Sunday, June 21.

Mr. and Mrs. Dionyious Braun took their daughter Isabel to Dickinson Monday where she will attend school for a few weeks.

Mr. and Mrs. Markus Franck and daughters and Miss Aurora Ternes will leave for Flasher Saturday. They expect to be home by Wednesday.

Quite a few farmers were at Linton last Saturday. They heard the speech given by Wm. Langer.

Mr. and Mrs. Leopold Schwahn were overnight visitors at the Anton Ternes place Sunday.

Farmers of this vicinity are busy working on the country roads.

6-1936

KRASSNA

By Rose Ternes

A few farmers motored to Burnstad Thursday, and on Friday Mike Fiest, Anton Ternes, John L. Baumgartner, Pete Biegler and Louis L. Welk took about 30 horses there to pasture them for a few months.

Mr. and Mrs. Max Tschosik and sons were Linton shoppers Saturday.

Mrs. Balzar Mattern and son Tony, Mrs. Louis Welk, Mrs. Anton Ternes and Mrs. Mike L. Welk, Eva and Julia Welk helped Mrs. Anna Mattern move Friday.

Pius Welk, who had been on the sick list the past few days, is recovering nicely.

Mr. and Mrs. John M. Ternes motored to Bismarck on a pleasure trip Saturday.

The schools in the Krassna district started Monday. Joe Biegler is teaching our school No. 1.

Mr. and Mrs. Nick Ternes and children and Otto Ternes are visiting friends in Solen over the weekend.

Peter, the 8 year-old-son of Mr. and Mrs. Wendelin Kramer was taken to Wishek. Peter is suffering with a sore foot.

Another WPA project was started yesterday near the Wendelin Kramer place.

EMMONS COUNTY RECORD

6-31-36

KRASSNA

By Rose Ternes

The young children of the Holy Trinity church received their first Holy Communion last Sunday. Rev. Father Eichner also announced that the children of this parish will be confirmed Sunday, July 5.

Miss Agnes Deringer worked for Mrs. Nick Ternes Friday and Saturday.

Frank A. Franck of Flasher will spend his summer vacation at the Markus Franck home.

This writer was injured badly Tuesday, June 23, when a cow stepped on her foot.

Sunday dinner guests at the Anton N. Ternes place were Mr. and Mrs. Anselm Sehn, Mr. and Mrs. Albert Jochim, Mr. and Mrs. George Deringer and Mr. and Mrs. Leopold Schwahn and family.

Mr. and Mrs. Joe Fiest and youngest son and daughter autoed to Minnesota last week.

Aloysius Mattern was working for Mike Welk last week.

Mr. and Mrs. Mike Burgad spent a few days at the Ben Biegler home.

This community was greeted with a nice rain Sunday morning, stopping the dust storms for a few days at least.

Mr. and Mrs. Louis Welk Jr. and family were visiting the Anton Ternes place Sunday night.

Nothing but politics has been going on for the last month. We hope it'll soon come to an end before some more fellows go "nuts."

7-9-1936

TIME HIGH RECORD
MERCURY JUMPS TO 116.5 HERE MONDAY

Last Hope of Any Crop Vanishes As Scorching Sun Blisters Prairie

Pushed upward by a blazing sun and scorching wind the thermometer jumped to an all time high record, reaching the 116.5 degree mark at the weather station in Linton Monday, as one of the most intense heat waves in the state's history swept North Dakota.

The sizzling temperatures which have ranged above the hundred mark for the past five days, have snatched from the drought stricken farmers their last flickering hopes of any salvage of their crops. There will not be a single bushel of small grain harvested in Emmons county.

Sunday the mercury jumped to 108 as a preliminary to Monday's record breaking performance. The intense heat has continued the wiping *Continued on next page*

105

EMMONS COUNTY RECORD

Continued from Previous Page

out of not only the wheat and small grain crop throughout western North Dakota but has ruined any feed crop which might have survived a normal dry period.

Along with the heat, hordes of grasshoppers have descended upon vegetation and in many cases stripped it clean. Farmers report cornfields and potato patches completely wiped out. Lacking anything to eat in the fields, swarms of the insects have swooped down upon city gardens to complete the picture of destruction.

Monday's high point in the state was at Fort Yates where the temperature reached 119. Napoleon and Jamestown each reported 118 degrees, Fargo 114, Valley City 115, Grand Forks 104, and Williston 110.

There was no report of persons stricken from the heat, but reports have come in of some Emmons livestock and hundreds of chickens dying from Monday's excessive temperature.

J.P. Munsch reported seven chickens dead and leaves of the trees shriveled up as though they had been hit by a heavy frost. Harry Nagel said along with many chickens, small birds had perished and thousands of hoppers had . . .

7-23-1936

KRASSNA

By Rose Ternes

Miss Annie Volk spent a few days visiting at her home last week.

Mr. and Mrs. Augustine Dirk of Selfridge were visiting old friends at Krassna Monday and Tuesday.

D. Braun, Jack Sehn and Ralph Shaffner left for Idaho Monday July 20. They expect to be home in about two weeks.

Many of the Krassna people were at Strasburg Tuesday night, July 14th. They attended the dance played by Lawrence Welk and his orchestra.

Mr. and Mrs. Ralph Shaffner and Mr. and Mrs. John Shaffner were Sunday dinner guests at the Anton Ternes place.

Mrs. Romanus Ternes has been seriously ill the past few days.

Mrs. Anna Mattern and family and Miss Eva Welk spent Monday visiting at the Anton Ternes place. Irene Mattern stayed out on the farm.

Pius Biegler can be seen driving a Chevrolet.

EMMONS COUNTY RECORD

8-20-1936

KRASSNA

By Rose Ternes

Mr. H. Tschosik is visiting old friends and relatives. He arrived at the Max Tschosik place Wednesday.

An ice cream social was held at the Krassna Store Sunday night. Those attending were Mr. and Mrs. D. Braun and family, Mr. and Mrs. Markus Franck, Mr. and Mrs. Nick Ternes, Mr. and Mrs. Anton Ternes, Miss Aurora Ternes and Miss Rose A. Ternes.

Mrs. Max Hiedrich celebrated her 50th birthday Wednesday night, Aug. 12. Many friends and relatives gathered.

Arthur Ternes is staying at the Romanus Ternes place while his parents, Mr. and Mrs. John Ternes, are visiting friends in Solen and Flasher.

Benny J. Welk of Ipswich, S. Dak. is visiting relatives in Strasburg and Krassna.

The D. Braun family is preparing for their auction sale which is to be held Saturday. They are moving to Coeur D'Alene, Idaho.

Miss Rigna Hientz, who had been working in Bismarck for several months is now visiting at the Tschosik place.

10-23- 1936

KRASSNA

By Rose Ternes

Mr. and Mrs. John L. Welk of Ipswich, S. D. arrived in Strasburg Sunday afternoon to take in the Strasburg fair and visit old friends and relatives.

Thursday afternoon another game of kitten ball was played by the Krassna school No. 2 and No. 3. No. 2 won.

Miss Anna Mary Deringer is working at the Wendeline Fischer place in town now.

Many of the Krassna folks attended the fair in Strasburg Sunday.

Little Annie Ternes, youngest daughter of Mr. and Mrs. Anton Ternes, was on the sick list last week.

Sunday Rev. Father Eichner invited all the members of the parish to the fair in the St. Bernard's church.

Wedding bells will soon be ringing for Fred Geotz and Miss Rigna Reinbold of Krassna; also for Matt Sherr of Strasburg and Ludwina Frison of Linton.

Steve Silvernagel moved his family and household goods to town this week.

KRASSNA

By Rose Ternes

Most of the farmers are done sowing wheat and are just starting to sow their barley and oats.

Johnny was working at the Max Tschosik place the past week.

Sheriff Langeliers was seen driving out in the Krassna vicinity Sunday.

Selma A. Ternes is helping Mrs. Markus Frank clean house this week.

Miss Aurora Ternes walked four miles to the Anton Ternes place Wednesday.

John Baumgartner has been very sick the past few weeks. He is at the hospital in Bismarck. Leo J. Baumgartner is helping Mike with spring work.

Mr. and Mrs. Ignatz Rienbold and family spent a few days in town with their mother Mrs. Peter Zacher, who has also been extremely ill.

Pupils of Krassna school No. 2, Mrs. Dornbush teacher, were in Linton last week.

Mrs. Ben Biegler has been on the sick list with rheumatism.

12-10-36

KRASSNA

By Rose Ternes

A little error was made in printing last week. A big crowd gathered to celebrate Mrs. Johnny "Schwahn's" namesday instead of Mrs. Johnny Schwab's.

The namesday Natalia was celebrated at the Wendelin Kramer place. Many friends were present.

Mr. and Mrs. John J. Tschosik were visitors at the Jake Fiest home last week Monday night.

Mrs. Balzar Mattern and son Myron spent a day at her home last week. Myron had been quite sick, but is alright again at this writing.

Wednesday while snowballing at school, Adam Tschosik hit Joe Biegler with a snowball with the result that his glasses were broken. This is the third pair of glasses Joe has had since school started.

I received a letter from the D. Braun family last week from Coeur D'Alene Idaho. They all like their new home and think they'll never want to live in North Dakota again.

EMMONS COUNTY RECORD

2-18-1937

KRASSNA

By Rose Ternes

Mrs. Pete Biegler worked at the Ben Biegler place Friday.

Mr. and Mrs. Wendelin Kramer were over-night visitors at the Balzar B. Mattern place one night last week.

Louis Welk Jr., Kasper Lipp and Anton Ternes took the train to Linton Friday night.

Nick Ternes got a load of groceries from Strasburg for the Krassna storekeeper last week.

Aloysius Mattern was an overnight visitor at the Anton Ternes place Friday.

I wonder if most of the readers read the last story in the Record "Too Soon to be a Bride". I sure think it was an interesting story and hope the next one will be the same.

Mr. and Mrs. Carl Gross are the parents of a baby girl. Mother and baby are fine.

Funeral services were held in the Holy Trinity church Saturday afternoon for the baby boy of Mr. and Mrs. Jack G. Biegler.

Ben Braun, George Deringer, John Kopp and several others drove to Linton with the sled Friday.

Mrs. Ignatz A. Reinbold, who had been ill and in town, returned to her home Thursday evening.

Mr. and Mrs. Markus Franck were visitors at the Anton Ternes place Monday night.

5-10-1937

KRASSNA

By Rose Ternes

Joe B. Beigler took three other boys to the western states last week.

Sunday, May 23, the Holy Trinity church of Krassna will celebrate its annual church feast. Services being at 8:30 and again at 10:30.

Max Heidrich and sons took livestock and machinery to Edgeley for Mrs. Joe Volk. Her two sons will take care of the livestock and put in a few acres of grain.

Mr. and Mrs. Rudolf Miller of Raleigh spent the week end visiting friends and relatives at Krassna.

Nick N. Ternes, Ben Braun, John and Romanus Schriner and Markus Franck left for Minnesota Monday morning.

Max Tschosik and Anton Ternes were business callers at Linton last week Friday. Pius Biegler suffered with a severe tooth ache last week.

EMMONS COUNTY RECORD

6-3-1937
KRASSNA
By Rose Ternes

Mr. and Mrs. Anton Reinbold motored to Raleigh and Shields Wednesday morning to spend a few days with relatives and friends.

A group of boys left for the western states last week to look for work.

Seventh and eighth grade students wrote examinations last week. Pupils of School No. 1 were Johnny Fiest, Balzar Kramer and Helen Tschosik.

Mr. and Mrs. Max Tschosik and Mr. and Mrs. Anton Ternes were callers at Hauge Sunday afternoon.

Miss Selma Ternes returned to her home last week.

The nice rain we had brought a big smile on every face.

Mr. and Mrs. Pius B. Biegler returned from their 8-day visit to Rosco, S.D.

9-4-1937
KRASSNA
By Rose Ternes

Mr. and Mrs. John and Adam Tschosik were on a business and pleasure trip to Fort Yates last week with the new car.

The Krassna school No. 1 kitten ball players hitch-hiked to school No. 2 Friday afternoon to show them how they can play. And did they show them! Score was 7 to 12 in favor of School No. 1.

Sebastian Sherr, Ray Braun and Aloysius R. Ternes, who spent several days in the eastern part of the state picking potatoes, returned last week.

Miss Alice Hager is again working at the Mike Fiest place.

Mr. and Mrs. George Dolinger visited at the Roy Ternes place Sunday.

1-1938
KRASSNA
By Rose Ternes

Nick Ternes has been very sick the last few days with the flu. A doctor was called Saturday and now lets hope he'll soon be on the road to recovery.

Several folks from around this vicinity spent New Year's day at the Anselm Sehn place to celebrate Mr. Sehn's birthday. Everybody had a nice time.

Everybody was shocked to hear of the sudden death which came to the well known Strasburg

Continued on next page

Continued from Previous Page

youth, Mike Senger. Sympathy is extended to the bereaved ones.

Sunday, while driving home from church, Max Tschosik and family had a little accident. Due to frosted windows, he ran into another car on the outskirts of town. However, nobody was injured.

Mrs. Ben Biegler, who has been sick and confined to her bed for several weeks is still in the same condition.

Last week the annual election was held and trustees again were elected for the St. Trinity church. George Deringer and Magnus Wagner were elected.

Selma Ternes spent her Christmas vacation at Mr. and Mrs. Markus Franck's place.

Mr. and Mrs. Melchoir Reil of Raleigh visited friends in Krassna and Strasburg a few days.

Mrs. Pauline J. Fiest, who is working at Bismarck, spent a few days at home.

1-1938

KRASSNA
By Rose Ternes

Mr. and Mrs. Wendelin Biegler and baby of Ft. Lincoln spent a few days visiting her parents, Mr. and Mrs. Ben Biegler.

Mr. and Mrs. John Ternes, Mr. and Mrs. Markus Franck and Mrs. Othillia Ternes drove to Bismarck

Friday to see John N. Ternes of Strasburg who is in the hospital there.

The writer spent a pleasant afternoon visiting Miss Tillie Baumgartner's school No. 2. I sure was interested in all the stories the students had to tell.

Oswald Ternes has a pretty good job now days, because he is working in the city.

Nick Ternes, who has been in bed has improved very much already.

Three Kings Day was spent in a very enjoyable way at many places.

EMMONS COUNTY RECORD

3-10-1938

KRASSNA
By Rose Ternes

Markus Franck and John N. Ternes made a business and pleasure trip to Mayville last week. They were expected home Wednesday this week.

The writer assisted Mrs. Markus Franck with her work while Mr. Franck was away.

A few young folks were at the Damian Baumgartner place Sunday, Feb. 27. All had a fine time.

Ben Braun and John Schriner made a trip to Oakes last week.

Romanus Ternes celebrated his namesday and birthday on Feb. ?? Several friends and relatives gathered at his home for the occasion.

A group of kids celebrated "fastnacht" at the Krassna store.

Mr. and Mrs. Ben Braun and Mr. and Mrs. Fred Goetz visited at the Mr. and Mrs. Markus Franck place.

A group of friends surprised Rose and Helen Ternes Sunday night at the Markus Franck place.

Mrs. Ignatz A. Reinbold, who had been in ill health is much better. She was seen in church Friday.

Last week some time Mr. and Mrs. Adam Schwab visited with their folks, Mr. and Mrs. George Deringer.

Mr. and Mrs. Nick Ternes and Aurora Ternes were callers at Linton and Strasburg.

November 3, 1938

KRASSNA
By Rose Ternes

Mrs. Wendelin Beigler of Fort Lincoln spent last week at the Pete Beigler place.

Mr. and Mrs. Joe Hager and Mr. and Mrs. Louis Welk spent Sunday night visiting at the Romanus Ternes place.

On Oct. 28, Lorraine Ternes, oldest daughter of Mr. and Mrs. Nick Ternes, celebrated her 6th birthday, and on Oct. 29, little Alvina, daughter of Mr. and Mrs. Markus Franck celebrated her 3rd birthday. Several friends gathered and the girls received many beautiful gifts.

Last week was a week of vacation for several CCC boys. They spent their time at their homes. Among them were Anton, Jake and Eugene Baumgartner, August Ternes and two Feist boys. They left again Sunday.

Not much news the last few days, but my saying is "no news is good news," especially for the correspondents and editors.

EMMONS COUNTY RECORD

December 22, 1938
KRASSNA
By Rose Ternes

Many friends and relatives gathered Dec. 13 to celebrate Mrs. Ottilia "Grandma" Ternes' namesday. She got many beautiful and useful presents.

Jake and Joe Holzer, who spent several weeks at home, are now at Aberdeen.

Tony M. Nagle stopped at the Krassna store Thursday night while on his way home from Linton. Says he'll make his home in Linton pretty soon.

St. "Christina" was celebrated at several different places on Dec. 15. Folks enjoyed the evening at Grandma Wolk's place.

Preparations are being made at Krassna School No. 1 for the Xmas program tomorrow night, Friday.

Mr. and Mrs. John Tschosik are the parents of a baby born to them Sunday. Mother and babe are at her mother's place at Hague.

Mr. and Mrs. Wendeline Biegler, who are spending a vacation at Krassna, motored to Bismarck Sunday.

Markus Franck celebrated his birthday Monday.

Dad has been on the sick list for several weeks suffering from severe stomach trouble.

A Merry Christmas to all the readers and editors of the Record.

January 26, 1939
KRASSNA
By Rose Ternes

Miss Barbara Mattern, who spent over a year in Minnesota, is now staying at the Louis L. Welk place.

Heard from my cousin, Isabel Braun of Coeur 'D Arlene, Idaho. She was married to Marvin Griffith Jan. 6. They are now on their way to New Hampshire. Brauns were former residents of Emmons County.

Several friends and relatives gathered to celebrate Sebastian Scherr's nameday, Jan. 2.

Mary Wolf, our school teacher, was an overnight visitor here last week.

Most everybody of around this locality has been having the flu.

EMMONS COUNTY RECORD

February 23, 1939
KRASSNA

SPORTS AND PLAY REPLACE POLICE AND JAIL IN CITY'S DRIVE TO SAVE YOUTH FROM CRIME

By Rose Ternes

A few friends gathered Thursday night at the Mike D. Fiest home to celebrate (Julia) Mrs. M. Fiest's namesday.

Mr. and Mrs. Anton Ternes were caller in Strasburg Sunday.

Due to bad roads and weather conditions, our teacher, Miss Mary Wolf of Hague, had to spend her last two week ends in Krassna.

Many had a hard time getting their surplus commodities the past week.

However, everybody to it and now have all the "Johnny cake" they want.

The writer returned home Tuesday after spending several days at the Markus Franck place.

10-3-1940
Krassna

By Rose Ternes

Mr. and Mrs. Ereth and son Donald of Solen had supper at the Anton Ternes place Saturday nite.

Mr. and Mrs. Max Tschosik and Mr. and Mrs. Anton Ternes made a pleasure trip across the river Sunday.

John M. Ternes local merchant, is taking over the Volk store in Strasburg this week.

The writer is first cook for the corn picking crew at the Markus Franck place.

Tony and Herman Brown are driving a different car now which they purchased last week.

EMMONS COUNTY RECORD

10-17-1940

KRASSNA

By Rose Ternes

Mr. and Mrs. Markus Frank and Mr. and Mrs. Nick Ternes assisted Mr. and Mrs. John Ternes in moving their household goods to Strasburg Monday.

Mr. and Mrs. Carl Gross are the parents of a baby girl, named Darleen. Sponsors were John Kapp and Miss Sybella Kramer. The latter spent a few days working there.

August Ternes started working in the North Side Pool Hall last week.

Oswald Ternes arrived in Strasburg unexpectedly Saturday nite. He had been in a CCC camp in South Dakota about 6 months.

Mrs. Carl Scherr is on the sick list.

Everybody went to town Monday nite to attend the wedding dance for Cecilia Unser and Johnny Reinbold.

November, 1940

KRASSNA

By Rose Ternes

A large crowd was present at the Krassna church Sunday to play bingo and other games. The church profited with good success.

Mr. and Mrs. Markus Frank and Rose Ternes left Monday to visit friends and relatives in Flasher. Cecilia is taking care of the farm and kids.

Adam Tschosik, was visiting with relatives in South Dakota, returned Friday.

Rose and Cecilia Ternes visited at the Nick Ternes place last week.

Quite a crowd gathered at Pete Braun's home to celebrate his birthday Monday nite.

Mr. and Mrs. Anton Ternes and Mr. and Mrs. Max Tschosik were Linton callers Monday.

Pete Biegler and family moved to the Ben Biegler farm last week.

Ann Ternes has been on the sick list for the last few days.

Angie Ibarra

12-5-1940

KRASSNA

By Rose Ternes

Tony Ternes spent a few days with Edwin Ternes this week.

Mr. and Mrs. George Deringer celebrated their 25th wedding anniversary Friday.

Mrs. Roy Ternes, who is sick and had been taken to the hospital, returned to her home Sunday. She is feeling fine now.

Joe Hager has been quite ill for the past week.

Rose Ternes is spending a few days at the Mike Welk place.

Mrs. Jake Selzler has been on the sick list this week.

Aloyse Ternes helped Markus Frank with some work Saturday.

Mr. and Mrs. John Tschosik and Ben Biegler were visiting with Ben Biegler Jr. in Firesteel, S.D. last week.

Mike Hummel helped Max Tschosik's with their butchering Wednesday.

Mr. and Mrs. Carl Gross from the Hague vicinity visited with friends in Krassna Sunday.

Little Joe Frank had the misfortune of falling from a chair and injuring his lower lip badly.

The lucky winners of the Krassna number books were Pius Hager, first, Ralph Brown, 2nd, and Tillie Ternes, 3rd.

4-10-1941

KRASSNA

By Rose Ternes

Mr. and Mrs. Max Tschosik and Mr. and Mrs. Anton Ternes visited friends in Bismarck last Thursday. They saw Mr. Hummel who is up and around after suffering with a sore leg. They also saw Anselm Sehn who is suffering with the barber's itch. He is improving, they say.

Miss Annamary Silvernagel, who had been in the St. Alexius hospital, returned to her home.

Mrs. George Deringer was taken to a hospital at Aberdeen. She is reported to be suffering from a tumor.

Miss Alice Welk visited here Sunday nite.

School No. 3 closed Monday with a party for the pupils.

Mr. and Mrs. Jake Schwahn are the parents of a baby girl born several days ago. The infant was named Bethann.

116

EMMONS COUNTY RECORD

5-12-1941

Krassna

By Rose Ternes

Miss Rose Reinbold is in a hospital at Bismarck. She is reported quite ill.

Joe Hager is in bed again and is seriously ill at this writing.

Mrs. Mike Welk was also on the sick list last week. Agnes Deringer is doing the household duties.

The writer had a pleasant visit with Agnes Kramer Sunday.

Grandma Ternes visited with us Sunday, also Mr. and Mrs. John Ternes of Strasburg.

Mrs. Therisia Hientz of Solen and Tony Hientz of Seattle, Wash. Visited at the Anton Ternes place Monday evening.

Mrs. Max Tschosik is at Hague with her sick father, Mr. Hummel. Selma Ternes is doing housework.

John Welk of Ipswich, S.D. visited friends near Strasburg, this week he was out here Monday.

7-17-1941

KRASSNA

By Lydia Ternes

Mr. and Mrs. Pius Biegler of Hazelton visited friends in Krassna Sunday.

Mr. and Mrs. John Ereth of Solen visited at the Max Tschosik place a few days.

Again farmers are losing horses from brain disease.

Pius Selzler, who spent a few months in an army camp, spent the fourth at home.

Jake F. Baumgartner is visiting friends at home after spending two years at Custer, S.D.

Friends were shocked to hear of the sudden death which came to the well known Mrs. John Kramer of near Linton. Sympathy is extended to the bereaved ones.

Mr. and Mrs. Max Tschosik made a trip to Bismarck last week Wednesday.

Among those to attend the dance at Mobridge Tuesday (music of Lawrence Welk) were: Mr. and Mrs. Mike Welk and Mr. and Mrs. Anton Ternes and Rose.

EMMONS COUNTY RECORD

7-24-41

Krassna

By Lydia Ternes

Ben Biegler who made a trip to the West Coast returned home. He saw his sons Joe and Wendlin and their families and the Dennyious Browns. They sent best regards to all their friends.

Pete Schwab and Max and Leo Baumgartner, who spent 4 months in an army camp in Wyoming, arrived home Saturday afternoon for a vacation.

Mt. and Mrs. Alex Scherr are working at the Joe Reinbold place.

Leo F. Baumgartner was a pleasant visitor and supper guest here Sunday.

Harvesting has begun in this community.

December 17, 1942

KRASSNA

By Rose Ternes

Mike Welk helped butcher at the Anton Ternes place Monday.

Selma Ternes visited in town a few days last week.

Mr. and Mrs. John Tschosik motored to Bismarck on Sunday.

The writer visited at the Nick Ternes place last week.

Mrs. Theresa Heintz from Hague and Miss Helen Tschosik helped butcher at the Mark Tschosik place Monday.

School No. 1 will present a Christmas program Tuesday, Dec. 22 at 8 P.M. Everyone welcome.

Fashions

Angie with her mother
and younger sister.
Angie is wearing her
favorite sailor dress.

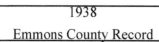

Fashions

Fashions are fads while style is timeless

Hats were a fashionable accessory for both men and women. Hats for women were generally trimmed with flowers, feathers or other decorations and were something most women could afford. Having a new hat for Easter, to wear to church, was almost essential. Another requirement for the hat was a hat pin. This was very popular and stylish in the earlier years but, with the unceasing wind in North Dakota, it was also a necessity. Some women wore bandannas rather than hats. The style in the 1930s and 1940s was to take a square bandana, fold it into a triangle, place the point on the top of the head, wrap the ends around from the nape of the neck, and tie it on the top, at the point. Other times it was worn as a triangle and tied under the chin or in back of the neck. Some older immigrant women wore black shawls, which they brought from Russia.

Women at the time wore their hair in waves. Finger waves were popular. A woman would place her finger on the hair she wished to wave and maneuver the hair between her fingers to create ridges, which would then form a wave. She could also use wave clips. They were of metal with a curved clip and a spring. These wave clips would be used to put a ridge on the top and bottom of a section of hair. Younger girls had ribbons and bows they wore in their hair. Hair nets were also a popular accessory.

Fedora style hats were worn by men and boys anytime they wore their suits. They would wear their hats when they went to church but always removed them in church or any other building. Men's hairstyles were more simplistic. Most men had their hair cut at home. Families had the equipment consisting of scissors, combs and clippers. A few people, especially businessmen in town, would go to the barber for a shave and a haircut.

The one-piece garments known as corsets, for women, consisted of a brassiere and girdle with garters and stays made of metal. This garment emulated armor, but it was something that women got used to wearing. By the late thirties, the separate bra and girdle had become acceptable, but one-piece corsets continued to be widely available.

Men usually had a suit to wear to church. The rest of the time they wore bib overalls. Wearing a suit to church was almost a requirement. The suits were made of wool and in the summer, without air conditioning, this was no small sacrifice.

An apron, worn over the dress, was everyday apparel for women, particularly for country women. It was usually made almost like a sleeveless dress, which tied in the back. It was more like a piece of equipment rather than a fashion statement. The skirt of the apron was used to carry anything from babies, eggs, firewood, or anything else that required carrying. Women did try to have their aprons look nice by trimming them with rickrack or other decorations.

Fur in the winter was becoming fashionable. My mother had a coat trimmed with a big fur collar. It frightened me when she wore it because my brother had convinced me it was a wolf.

In winter the children wore long underwear with buttons up the front and a flap in back. The girls also wore long stockings over the underwear. They came in one color, brown, and were always wrinkled. They were usually held up with rubber bands with the top rolled over the bands. Since elastic bands were not always available, other rubber items were used such as rubber rings from canning jars.

During the war rubber was in short supply, therefore elastic was not readily available. Buttons were substituted for undergarments requiring elastic. The zipper became popular during the 1930s and was known as a "slide fastener." B. F. Goodrich coined the name "zipper" and used it as a fastener on overshoes. The zipper became popular for children's clothing and men's trousers in the 1920s and 1930s. Dresses often had zippers down the back, which required major contortionist skills or the help of another person to zip it up. With the advent of slacks for women the zipper was used as a side fastener.

In the 1930s the DuPont Company introduced nylon stockings but the war interrupted the sale of them since nylon was needed for making parachutes. The stockings had a black seam up the back.

Keeping seams straight was a full time job. When nylons became unavailable during the war the more stylish younger women would draw a black line up the back of their legs to imitate the stocking seam.

Angie and Johanna her younger sister

Most people in the rural areas had only two pairs of shoes. The children in the area usually went barefoot in the summer. Walking barefoot in the mud after the rain was a very sensual feeling with the mud squishing between their toes. One pair of shoes was used for everyday wear or working. The other pair was for dress. These shoes were for dances and going to church. When the heels or soles wore out they were repaired at home. A piece of equipment used to repair shoes was a metal stand with a top that was a replica of a foot. Metal tips prevented heels from wearing out so fast. Those were a half moon shape with holes premade for pounding in the nails.

Polishing shoes was a Saturday night ritual. The whole family's shoes were polished and shined for church on Sunday. Sometimes this duty fell to the younger members of the family. This was no easy task, as the only shoe polish available was a paste wax polish. During cold and snowy weather rubber galoshes (boots) were worn. They fastened up the front with metal buckles.

In the G/R community nothing was wasted or thrown away. Most women sewed and made clothing for the family. My mother was blind in one eye due to a cataract, so did not do much sewing. We did have a Singer pedal sewing machine and I learned to sew doll clothes at a young age, as soon as I could reach the pedal.

Another source for getting clothing was through the Sears or Montgomery Ward's catalog. That catalog was used to buy almost

123

anything that was not available in town. We were the purveyors of recycling. When the new catalog came out the old one was used for toilet paper, unless you had tissue from fruit wrappings. The best tissue was wrapped around peaches.

In Linton, at the J C Penney's store, they had a section on one wall that had children's clothes. Many of the clothes were sailor or army suits or sailor dresses for girls. I can remember seeing a little sailor dress which I coveted. My mother had someone sew my sister and me a dress like it

After the war, when clothing was a little easier to get, the older schoolgirls would wear cardigan sweaters, which they would turn around and button down the back. Since there was no TV and no shopping centers, Sears and Ward's was our inspiration for fashions. It was pure entertainment to look through the catalog and see all the beautiful luxurious things and let yourself imagine that you lived that lifestyle. Some items were bed jackets trimmed with lace and dresser sets on a mirror-tray which included a hairbrush, hand held mirror, comb and a container for powder. It was as much fun to look at these items in the catalog as to own them.

Cleanliness was also part of the G/R tradition. True to the German traditions everything was structured including washing and ironing. Clothes were usually washed on Mondays. This required a good deal of work as water had to be carried in and boiled on the cook stove for clothes to be washed. In order to make the white clothes even whiter, bluing was put in the rinse water. Clothes were hung on the line in a structured fashion. Clothing and other items were hung in categories, which was almost an art form.

Washable, easy-care fabrics were introduced in

Mother hanging clothes to dry.

the 1930s. An advertisement in the Sears catalog read: "USE LUX: We advise gentle LUX for best results in washing these clothes." Although, in the 1930s, these fabrics were not yet introduced to the rural farming community of Krassna.

Going to the store to pick up soap for washing clothes was also not reasonable, especially when the roads were closed most of the winter. In order to have soap for the year the early settlers made their own. This was part of the butchering process where nothing was wasted. Lard from the animal that was not used for cooking was used to make soap. Making soap consisted of lye and lard. However, once again you did not go to the store to buy the lye. You made your own. Lye was made with ashes from wood, which was used to heat the house and for cooking. This required a process where hot water would be poured over the ashes, usually put into a wooden barrel, with a drain hole. The liquid produced from this process was lye. We had an ash pile by our house used for making lye. After the lard and lye were combined they would be poured into a container and when hardened would be cut into squares or other shapes. This required some skill, because if you used too much lye the soap would be too strong for washing and irritate your skin.

Tuesday was ironing day. The iron was heated on the stove, or some people had gas irons with a little tank attached to keep the iron hot. Clothes were sprinkled, usually using a water-filled empty ketchup bottle with a metal stopper. A cork attached on the bottom of the stopper fit into the bottle. Little holes on the metal stopper top sprinkled out the water. The clothes were sprinkled then rolled up to keep them damp. This made it easier to iron out the wrinkles, especially since most fabrics were made of cotton. Almost everything that was washed needed ironing. Sheets and pillowcases, which only came in white, also had to be ironed. Handkerchiefs were ironed. Kleenex was not yet available. Having a fancy handkerchief was fashionable. Sometimes you got one as a gift, decorated with embroidery or lace, which of course needed ironing.

After the war everything changed, including fashions. Cars became popular. The roads were better and Krassna was no longer an isolated community.

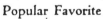

Food

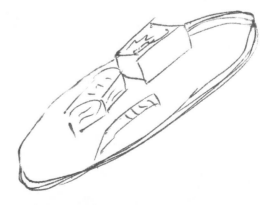

Angie Ibarra

Food

Schmeckt gut (Tastes Good)

The Germans from Russia who lived in Krassna had a very unique cuisine. Although the cooking remained predominately German, it evolved over a period of time, since the Germans moved around to different countries and continents. In Germany they lived in a region where forests and woodlands were abundant. In Russia they lived by the Black Sea, where they raised apricots and grapes and picked up some of the Russian's ways of preparing food. One example was watermelon in brine to make watermelon pickles,

German restaurant food would be quite different from the food of the G/R. Likewise, in a Russian restaurant G/Rs would not recognize most of the food. When our ancestors came to North Dakota they had to adapt again, because the ingredients that were available in Germany or Russia were not readily available on the prairie. The climate in North Dakota was much colder then it was by the Black Sea in Russia.

The G/Rs were exposed to other ethnic groups that lived in surrounding countries. The Jewish, Polish and Romanian culture also contributed to the G/R cuisine. Although, Krassna was a very rural community the G/Rs ate food that was imported from the Middle East. Examples were Halvah and Greek olives that were popular. These foods are now considered gourmet foods with a price to match.

When I was a child I never really liked Halvah. It seemed like we had it on the table continually. It was a very good snack made from sesame seeds and honey.

The other signature G/R food, kuchen, can be served as a dessert or as a snack. It is made of bread dough or non-yeast dough topped with fruit filled custard. Variations stirred into the custard include prunes, peaches, cottage cheese, or just sugar and cinnamon.

Homemade noodles, golden drops in chicken soup, sprinkled

with aromatic cinnamon, were frequently on the menu, particularly for Sunday dinner. Creamed chicken was often served as well. It was like a chicken fricassee, chicken cooked with cream called *rahm dunkus*, cream dunker. You would break off pieces of bread and scoop up the cream, using the bread in your hands.

One time we went to visit relatives who were more sophisticated then we were. They served the dish with forks to skewer the bread and dunk it into the cream. They also had napkins by each place setting. We did not use napkins, as it would have been a lot of work to launder and iron them. Paper napkins were not readily available.

Making the homemade noodles was quite a job. After the dough was made, pillows would be placed on the back of chairs and covered with clean dish towels. Then the thin noodle dough would be placed on the dish towels and left to dry. The noodles would then be cut into strips. Later they would be cooked and made into various dishes.

Another type of soup served frequently was borscht. It was a Russian beef soup with a lot of beets. The G/R had their own version by adding cabbage, barley, carrots and potatoes topped with a dollop of sour cream.

A dessert dish that is not very well known outside of the G/R community is citron. It is like a melon but needs to be cooked to be edible. The G/R cooks prepared it with raisins, water and sugar.

Because fresh fruit was hard to come by, especially in the winter, dried food was used. Many food dishes were made with raisins, such as raisin cream pie, which I disliked. Raisins were also put into sweet rolls and cookies. I refused to eat raisins so picked them out when they were in my food.

Out on the prairie we ate breakfast, dinner, and supper. This was one of the more difficult terms to get used to after we left Krassna. In cities people ate breakfast, lunch, and dinner.

Breakfast on the farm consisted of leftovers. We usually had sausage, kuchen, and even cake along with other leftovers. At noon dinner was the big meal, while supper might be a lighter meal. I learned fast when I was grown and had roommates. One morning we were out of food for breakfast. I volunteered to go to the corner store. I brought back chocolate cake. My roommate thought that was hilarious. I, however, did not think it was an unusual breakfast item.

Places to store preserved food before refrigeration came to the farm consisted of indoor and outdoor cellars. We kept food such as pickled watermelon rind, other pickles, and sauerkraut in brine in the indoor cellar. These items were placed in a crock with a stone on top to keep pickles or kraut submerged. Canned meat such as chicken, beef, pork, and sausage, as well as canned tomatoes, green beans, and a number of other preserved foods that required a cool environment were also kept there.

The outdoor cellar, which was typical G/R architecture, was a building that was high in the front to accommodate a full sized door and slanted down to the ground in the back. It was usually white washed. The outdoor cellar was cool in the summer and warm enough to not freeze in the winter. Root foods such as carrots, beets and potatoes were kept there, as were blocks of ice that my dad cut from the Missouri river. The ice was covered with flax straw, which was more dense then regular straw. The ice would stay frozen until the middle of summer. It was a very dark place and I avoided going down there.

In Krassna most people had a summer kitchen. This was a separate building with a kerosene cook stove where food was prepared. The reason for the summer kitchen was that it was too hot to cook in the house since there was no air conditioning. Heating up the house was not what you wanted to do especially since North Dakota had such hot summer temperatures. We built a new house just before I was born. It was a split level with the kitchen in the lower level, so I missed out on the summer kitchen.

Butchering was a big event that would qualify as a celebration because usually several people came to your house to help. They would stay to eat. Some of the men were skilled for specialized parts of the butchering process, such as killing the animal. Others were skilled sausage makers. Butchering required a lot of preparation and had to be done in cooler weather. Wood had to be gathered to keep the water in the big kettle heated. The children helped by keeping the wood supplied. Every part of the animal was used; the lard was used for soap, cooking and poured over the sausage to seal and preserve it. The scrap meat was used to make headcheese. The feet were pickled along with the gelatin extracted from the feet. Some of the meat was put into smoke house where it was smoked. Some of the meat was canned. The meat had to be preserved to last until the next butchering event.

In the summer jars of coffee with milk and sugar were kept in the horse water tank to keep them cool. Again we were way ahead of the times. Now a similar coffee at a coffee shop is very pricey. Children were also allowed to drink the coffee, which was mostly milk.

The G/R had a tradition of planting two gardens. One was the vegetable garden with the root vegetables and the *Bashtan* that consisted of rows of sweet corn and vine vegetables such as succulent watermelons and cantaloupes. Other vine crops were pumpkins, squash, and potatoes. The potatoes required a lot of work as they attracted potato bugs. Getting rid of the bugs was often a family gathering. In the evening the whole family would gather to pick the bugs off of the potatoes and put them in a can filled with kerosene, thus meeting their demise.

Watkins products purchased from the Watkins man were kept in the pantry. These included spices like cinnamon, nutmeg, and allspice, extracts such as lemon flavoring, as well as all of the things needed for baking and cooking were in the pantry. Homemade ice cream made in a hand cranked ice cream freezer was the ultimate treat. The flavors were wonderful because of Watkins extracts and flavors such as vanilla and, my favorite, maple.

The appearance of the "Watkins man" was a welcome event as he brought more than just spices to his customers. He was one of the few links to the outside world. He brought news about the surrounding neighbors out on the desolate prairie. He brought the latest national and world event news, the going price for wheat and other grains, the birth of a new baby, the illness of anyone on his route and any other titbits of communication. He was invited for meals and often to stay the night. Having a visitor during the week was an enjoyable occasion.

Sunflower seeds known as Russian peanuts were also grown on the farm. When you had company everyone would sit around and eat sunflower seeds and talk. We would simply put newspapers on the floor and everyone would eat to their hearts content and spit the shells on the newspapers. This was a great story telling time. Stories were told with a lot of drama. This was a real learning experience for the younger children.

We even made our own root beer. I remember the metal stand we used to put the bottles under to snap on the caps. Bottles such as ketchup bottles were saved for making root beer.

We made our own candy and sometimes-even gum. When you took a handful of wheat and chewed it, it became like dough and could be used like gum. Homemade wine was another staple made from various available ingredients. Other snacks were cabbage cores. Because the GRs made a lot of sauerkraut and also ate a lot of cooked cabbage these were common treats. I still enjoy eating cabbage cores.

We used to store brown sugar in the attic. I loved the taste of brown sugar so I would go up to the attic and eat it. It was like candy. Somehow a silver marble was stuck under the eaves. My brother told me it was a lion and that was his eye, so I stopped going to the attic to eat brown sugar.

We also raised our own popcorn. We used to pop corn and tried to get a lot of old maids. My brother and I would grind them up in a coffee grinder add a little oil and salt and it was a taste delight. We would also use the leftover popped popcorn for cereal. It is very good with milk and sugar.

Some other snacks were Sen Sen to sweeten your breath and Black Jack or Clove chewing gum. One time when my older brother had gone to town he bought me a bag of potato chips. I thought it was one of the best things I ever ate. They were a new food that had not yet reached the prairie.

We were a self-sufficient group. We had animals to supply the meat and milk for drinking, baking, and making cheese and ice cream and the gardens to supply vegetables. Most of the GRs made homemade cottage cheese. It would be hung in flour sacks with a pan underneath to catch the drippings. After it was fermented it was fried in a pan and the crust it left was a very tasty snack.

We usually had very good meals in spite of the dust bowl and war because we lived on a farm and grew most of our own food. Shopping for most farmers usually consisted of a sack of flour, a sack of sugar, and coffee. Almost everything else was grown and preserved for later use. The store that was part of the community, but closed before I was born, had a large shed built onto it just to store flour. Most G/R dishes required flour.

Angie Ibarra

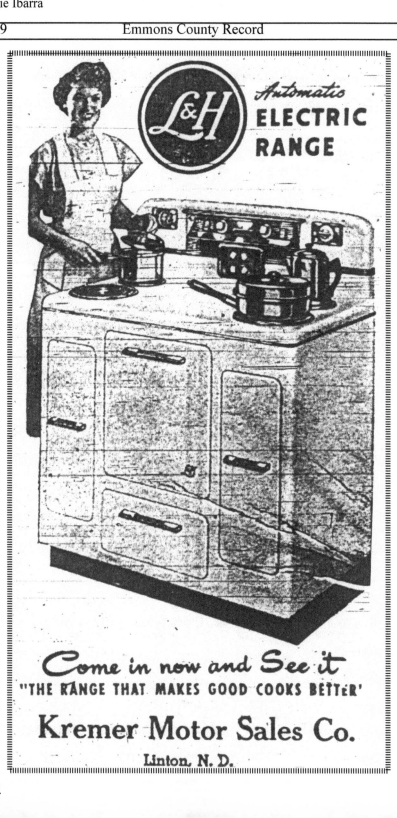

Flour-Sack Underwear

When I was a Maiden fair,
Mama made our underwear.
With five tots and Pa's poor pay,
How could she buy us lingerie?

Monograms and fancy stitches
were not on *our* flour-sack britches...
Panty waists that stood the test
With "Gold Medal" on the Chest.

Little pants, the best of all,
With a scene I still recall:
Harvesters were gleaning wheat
Right across the little seat.

Tougher than a grizzly bear
Was our flour sack underwear...
Plain or fancy, three feet wide,
Stronger than a hippos hide.

Through the years each Jill and Jack
Wore this sturdy garb of sack.
"Waste not, want not," we soon learned;
"Penny saved, a penny earned."

Beadsspreads, curtains, tea towels too;
Tablecloths to name a few.
But the best beyond compare,
Was our flour-sack underwear.

*Printed with permission from DRG, publisher of
"Old-Time Art of Thrift," the book in which this poem was printed.
DRGNetwork.com*

Games and Toys

Angie's brother Lawrence

Angie and her sister Johanna

Toys and Games

Fun and games depended on ingenuity and imagination

The G/R children had to be creative and inventive in playing when they were not working. Out on the prairie there were no parks, no play equipment and not many store-bought toys. This must be fascinating to today's younger generation who can't imagine living with out texting or having television with unlimited stations, or video games.

In the winter when my dad worked in the shed cutting things out of wood he would also cut out blocks of wood so I could build things. One of my favorite toys was a wooden horse that he made for me out of a broomstick. It had a horse's head that he had carved. I would ride all over the farmyard with my horse. My ambition in life was to be a cowgirl. I guess I was inspired by the few movies I saw. One of the first movies I saw was a western. It had a scene with a little girl who fell off of a horse. It affected me very much, causing me to be in a sad emotional state for some time. I related movies with reality, not knowing the difference.

When I was not riding my horse, I enjoyed playing with dolls and even dressing up the cat and dog. I think they appreciated the attention. We had a German shepherd named Robert. I don't know how he got that name. He was a very good guard dog, but was also gentle when I played with him.

I had several dolls, one was a rubber doll which my brothers took apart and used

Angie and her doll

149

the head for a baseball. The doll had the name of the company who made it stamped on the back. I once asked my mother why we had letters on our backs. She had no idea what I was talking about, until I showed her the stamp on my rubber doll. I can't remember her exact explanation, other than that was just stamped on dolls and not on our backs.

I learned how to use the pedal Singer sewing machine at an early age and loved designing and sewing clothes for my dolls. One time while visiting my cousins in Strasburg I played with the girl across the street. We designed doll houses and used dolls made out of clothespins wearing various garments. I also enjoyed embroidery. Another thing I loved to do, when we went to Linton where they had a Penny's store, was to look at dolls with my dad. My mother and little sister would shop for needed items, while my dad would take me to look at the dolls. I didn't necessarily want to buy them, I was happy to just look at them.

I honed my culinary skills early when I would go down by our orchard. It had a variety of weeds and a few trees growing there. I would whip up all kinds of dishes using the weeds and also made mud pies. I loved making mud pies in the discarded cookware I found in our junk yard, a little distance from the house. It had all sorts of junk that could be used creatively, thus inspiring my love for junk yards to this day.

Playing school and church was something else I did occasionally. When I played church I always played the part of a priest, which seemed more interesting than being a nun who, it seemed to me, just prayed. I didn't play church very often as I only had my little sister as my congregation. After giving the sermon and the blessing there wasn't much else that I knew how to do with the church service. My sister got bored with my sermons. I also played school but, again, my sister was my only student along with the cat, dog and my dolls.

There were no playmates close by as farms were too far apart. Many people had large families and the children automatically had playmates. Our family consisted of 5 at one time. My mother had a couple of miscarriages that really fragmented our family. My oldest sister had a brain tumor and died at 18 when I was four. That left me with my two brothers. One was eleven years older and one five years older then I. My sister was two years younger.

Although we did not have TV or video games or very many other toys, we found ways to entertain ourselves. We would often go up to the attic where old clothes were stored and play dress up. I made and decorated a little room up there. I enjoyed interior designing as well as clothes designing. When the granaries were not in use I used one for a playhouse. I loved to do interior decorating in my playhouses, inspired by the Sears and Ward catalogs.

We were not supposed to play in the barn, so didn't. There were smaller animals roaming the yard. We had a sheep that was born the same day that I was born. I used to ride her when not riding my wooden horse. She was a tolerant creature. Chickens and roosters also roamed the yard. I was frightened to death of the chickens, particularly the rooster, who chased anyone when he had a chance, instilling a fear of fowls in me to this day.

I had a red rubber car which I called my Ford, don't know why, as we never owned Fords. Sometimes when my dad went to town he would come home with presents for us. One time he bought my sister and me each a little red chair. When I was about five he bought me a tricycle. Another toy that I enjoyed was a metal windmill. You would pour water in the bottom tray attached to it and the turning blades pumped water. I thought that was very scientific. When not playing with my toys I played on the swing next to our house.

My brothers also had toys. My youngest brother wanted an army set. However, my parents did not like the idea of him playing a game related to the war, but did finally get him the game. Almost all young boys had jack knives that they used for any number of things. They also made slingshots, a good practice for eye hand coordination, when shooting rocks. Trying to make a perfect sling shot was an accomplishment worth pursuing. Slingshots could be used for a variety of things, such as a toy or a weapon. Whistling also seems to be a lost art today. You don't hear boys doing much whistling anymore, probably because iPods are now used for music and you can text instead of calling someone by whistling.

In the winter we played Fox and Geese at school, along with snowball fights and skating on the ice, without ice skates. My brothers and neighbor kids went sledding on the hill on our farm. They used tires, inner tubes, grain shovels and anything found on the farm that would slide down the hill.

In the summer my brother and I made boats out of wood and sailed them in a ditch filled with water. We could find any number of ordinary things that could be creatively used as a toy.

1929	Emmons County Record

4-4-1929

FORT YATES INDIAN'S SCALP LINTON NINE
Start Warfare in Fifth Inning -- Whites Weak with Nine Errors

The Redskins from across the river representing the Fort Yates baseball team are on the warpath.

Sunday, especially in the fifth inning, when they bombarded the white men's defense with the horse hide which they were unable to handle, and right then and there took Linton's scalp. Scoring five runs, as a result of five errors and three hits. They had scored two runs previously on an error and two hits.

Pius served him up for Linton but the Red's liked this hot stuff and got to his offerings quite freely. Of course it would have been different had his teammates given him tighter support. Lipp relieved Pius in the sixth and pitched shutout ball for four innings.

The local team hit just four times more than the Indians but were unable to make them count it. A little birdie told us there

was some mighty poor base running on the part of the locals. T. Volk, Schwartz and Koeppen were out of the lineup Sunday, all being out of town.

The results of scorer Chuck Lang's efforts follows:

	AB	R	H	E
LINTON	41	6	9	9
FORT YATES	35	7	5	8

Health and Medicine

Health and Medicine

An apple a day keeps the doctor away.
- English proverb

Krassna was located in an isolated area. The closest town was Strasburg, which was about ten miles away. Hospitals or doctors were not readily available. A country doctor was called on for extreme emergencies and arrived in his horse and carriage.

Childbirth was usually not an extreme emergency; therefore, most of the children were born at home. Women friends or relatives would help with the delivery, or the doctor would help if the pregnancy had been problematic.

I chose to enter the world the year North Dakota had very extreme temperatures. That year the thermometer ranged between 120 degrees above zero and 60 degrees below. I was born in 1936. The 120 degrees above zero registered on the day I was born was probably the hottest day of the century. There was no air conditioning and fans could not be plugged in since there wasn't any electricity. We had a generator and usually had electricity when I was young, depending on the wind, but probably did not have it when I was born. Most families were large. Ten to fifteen children were not uncommon, as they were needed to help on the farm. Childbirth was a frequent occurrence.

Some of the nearby villages had specialized doctors. Eureka had an optometrist for eye glasses. I had glasses when I was very young, so went to Eureka to get them. Wishek had a chiropractor and Linton had a dentist. I have fond memories of going to Linton to see the dentist. We would stop at a restaurant, probably the only one in town. The beef sandwiches on store-bought white bread, was in itself a treat, with a round mound of potatoes in the center with gravy covering the bread and potatoes. This is still one of my favorite dishes.

I thought the dentist used clippers to pull teeth as to me they looked like the clippers my dad used to cut my brother's hair. I had very bad toothaches when I was a child, which is probably why we went to the dentist. However, in most cases, if a tooth needed to be pulled you would simply tie a string around the offending tooth and pull. Sometimes you would tie the end of the string to a doorknob and slam the door and it would come out. There also were no tooth fairies on the prairie. I don't believe they ever heard of Krassna, North Dakota, or at least it wasn't on the tooth fairy route. The reward was getting rid of the offending tooth.

Other remedies were obtained from the Watkins man who came around winter and summer. Going to town before cars were popular was a major event, particularly in the winter when the roads were snowed under, sometimes for months at a time.

Watkins products were used everywhere on the farm, for people as well as animals. There was a liniment used for horses and a particular for people to use for backaches. Watkins Petro Carbo Salve was a common product used for cuts and bruises and everything in between. Store bought items were Iodine and Mercurochrome. Iodine left brownish, reddish spots on the cuts or bruises and really burned when applied. Mercurochrome is no longer used as it contains mercury. Kerosene was another remedy used for a variety of aches and pains.

The Germans from Russia settlers all had their home remedies which they used to treat whatever aliment the person had. The home remedies were made from common herbs, kitchen food supplies and items readily available in the pioneer grocery store. Peppermint, which was also called green drops, had an age-old reputation for relieving upset stomach and heartburn. We would put peppermint on a spoonful of sugar. Peppermint burned when taken. To this day I still get a stomach ache just thinking about it. Another remedy for an upset stomach was to mix soda and vinegar together then drink it while it was bubbling. A relief for the pain from burns was Unguentine Ointment.

Chamomile tea was another common pain reliever. In the summer chamomile plants grew wild. We would pick the little white daisy-like blossoms. They were placed on a clean cloth to dry then used for making tea. It had many health properties such as reducing stress, promoting sleep and reducing inflammation.

Other common cure-alls included castor oil, which most parents gave to their children. It was disliked by most. I, however, liked it, probably the only person in the world who did. I enjoyed the fish taste.

I was a sickly child who grew into a very healthy adult. Therefore, I was the subject of many home remedies. Like most of the prairie children I had common childhood diseases such as scarlet fever, chicken pox, measles, ringworm and pink eye.

I was not one to take anyone's word for anything and usually tended to try out things for myself. We used to get dressed by the cook stove in the winter, as it was the warmest place in the house. One morning my mother told me not to sit on the oven door, as it was too hot. I sat on it anyway. I am sure I had to have many applications of Unguentine Ointment. I also had to sit on pillows for some time. Another time I swallowed a bullet that passed through my system, probably with the help of castor oil.

Angie and Johanna by the poultry house.

Emmons County Record

1935	1935

1960	Emmons County Record

Religion

Religion

God is our refuge and strength

Psalms 46:1

The touchstone of these industrious G/R pioneers was their deep religious faith. Even after experiencing hardships such as the long frigid winters, the extreme hot summers, loneliness, dust storms, draught, grasshoppers, crop failures and many other difficulties, their faith continued unimpaired.

The new church, Holy Trinity Catholic Church, was built in Krassna in 1916. Previously, from 1901, the congregation had been a mission, housed in an old building, which later became a community hall. The old building was used for catechism classes, school plays, basketball and a place for the altar boys to change into their altar boy attire.

There was also a barn and two outdoor outhouses. Even when cars were more accessible people still arrived at the church with their horses and buggies, especially when the roads were impassible. Other times students would ride their horses to catechism classes.

The priests who served the parish were The Reverends:
Bernhard Eichner, September 1915 to September 1941.
John A Selder, September 1941 to Aug. 1961,
later became a monsignor.
John a Dubsky, August 1961 to November 1962.
The Reverend Peter Goeser of Sts. Peter and Paul Church,
Strasburg, North Dakota offered the last Mass July 30, 1967.

Holy Trinity Catholic Church was torn down after being empty for some years. Some of the ornamental statues from the church were placed in the cemetery that is still in existence today.

In the sanctuary church goers were separated by gender. The men sat on the right side of the church and the women on the left. The children, who were old enough, sat in the front rows. One time when I was quite young I wanted to sit with my dad, thinking it might be more exciting. I must have misbehaved because I remember the man behind me shaking his finger at me. I wasn't used to anyone scolding me, so after that I went with my mother. I sat with her until I was old enough to go to the front pew with the other children. I had trouble remembering which hand was used to make the sign of the cross. So my mother, in her wisdom, bought me a bracelet to wear on my right hand.

I remember going with my dad to the priest's house to subscribe to the "Children's Messenger." I loved reading it, as it was one of the few pieces of reading material we had in the house. I don't recall what was in it, but it did have children's stories.

Some winter days when a teacher from Strasburg was unable to make it out to the country to teach, the priest would come over and teach at the school. The parish house was located very close to School Number 3.

Church was the big social event of the week. We would arrive early, before mass to visit with our neighbors. The church service was usually quite lengthy and lasted until noon. This was during the period when the Catholic Church had high and low Latin masses. The High Mass consisted of a lot of singing, and the sermons were long. It was also much more formal. When communion was served the altar boys would put up a communion cloth similar to a tablecloth and only the priest would give communion. The altar boys would hold a gold plate-like device under each person's chin while receiving communion. The priest would preach about hell and damnation and you certainly did not want to end up there. These sermons contributed to the formation of a consciousness that kept most of the pioneers on the straight and narrow. After all that you would go to someone's house for dinner, or people would come over to your house for dinner and visit, because Sundays were visiting days. However, the cows still had to be milked and some work had to be done, but work was kept to a minimum on Sunday.

Funerals were usually a three-day event. My sister Rose died from a brain tumor at age 18. I was only four. This was in May 1941. She was one of the first patients operated on for a brain tumor at Mayo Clinic in Rochester, Minnesota. After she died her body was brought home for a wake and burial. I remember standing by the window where sheets of rain splashing against the glass were merging with my tears, my father was talking to me and telling me that she was in heaven. My brother informed me years later that I kept going to the coffin, which was on a piano bench in our living room and touching her. She was like my second mother. After the wake the coffin was placed on the pickup truck and taken to the church and later the cemetery. It was a very bleak day.

My sister's death was a great loss for my parents and particularly stressful for my dad. During her hospitalization he had frequently traveled back and forth to Rochester. When she came home in the coffin, he went by horse and buggy to meet the train in Strasburg. My mother was at home with 4 younger children, plus it was planting season. The hardship was almost unbearable. I do remember that we were very sheltered after that event.

Another memorable death was when lightning struck a farm family while they were out in the barn doing the milking chores. They were all standing in a row when the lightning bolt hit the father and one of the girls. The father was knocked unconscious and the daughter was killed instantly. The wife accompanied her husband to the hospital in Bismarck. Due to lack of transportation and no phone service, the daughter's funeral had to be held without the mother being able to attend.

When there was a thunderstorm out on the barren prairie it was intense. Lightning flashed and thunder roared and rain came down in droves. It was not a place for the faint of heart to live. My mother would walk around the house with a bottle filled with holy water and sprinkle holy water in every room. We were not allowed to eat until the storm had passed because the silverware might conduct electricity. Almost everything came to a halt until the storm was over.

The G/R were very religious in other ways as well. Prayers were recited before and after meals asking for God's blessing and thanking God afterwards for the meal while standing up with your hands folded. During Lent, the Rosary was recited each evening. Prayers were said before going to bed while kneeling down by the bed.

Other signs of religious devotions were shrines that almost every

G/R in Krassna had situated in a corner of the living room. The shrine consisted of a statute of Jesus and a statute of the Blessed Virgin Mary and sometimes other religious ornaments.

The church, as a center of the community, provided a stability that knitted the people together. This socioeconomic observance is still a work in progress. The deep faith and spiritual life is probably what helped the early settlers get through all their hardships.

Holy Trinity Catholic Church

d Church now Community Hall

EMMONS COUNTY RECORD
OFFICIAL NEWSPAPER OF EMMONS COUNTY AND CITY OF LINTON

9-8-1965

Msgr. John A. Selder

Shown above is an Emmons County Catholic clergyman who was recently granted honors by Pope Paul V1. He was named domestic prelate, with the title of Right Reverend Monsignor, according to an announcement by Bishop of Bismarck Hilary B. Hacker.

Msgr. John A. Selder, presently pastor of St. Michael's Church and dean of the Hague Deanery, was born in Germany in 1883. He completed his clerical studies at the University of Freiburg in Switzerland in 1916 and was then ordained. He came to the Bismarck in 1921 after which he served churches at Hoff, Fallon Grenora and Flasher.

In 1941 he came to Emmons County as pastor of Holy Trinity Church in the Krassna community and served that church until he was transferred to St. Michael's in 1961.

11-1962

Krassna Priest, 54 Found Dead at Home

The Rev John Dubsky, 54 pastor of Holy Trinity Catholic Church in the Krassna District southwest of Strasburg, was found dead in his home early Friday morning, the victim of an apparent heart attack. He had apparently died early Thursday evening.

According to those familiar with his activities he had enjoyed a successful deer hunt Thursday afternoon, had brought the deer home and with the assistance of a neighbor, Leo Unser, had hung the carcass in the garage. He declined an invitation for coffee at the Unser home saying he did not feel well. He then went in the house and that is the last time anyone saw him alive.

Father Dubsky had scheduled a 6 a.m mass in the living room of his house for Friday, but when Mrs. Rose Unser, who lives nearby, arrived Friday morning, she noticed some lights on in the house. She entered, but no one appeared so she begin looking about. When she went up the stairs to the second floor, she noticed Father Dubsky's body where he had collapsed near or in the bathroom. It is believed he had been dead for about 12 hours.

Not much is known of Father Dubsky's early life, but it is known that he was born May 31, 1908 in Czechoslovakia and that he grew up and was educated there. He managed to escape from behind the iron curtain and arrived in the United States in April 1951. Since coming to this country he had served parishes in Amidon, Dickenson, Devils Lake, New Lepzig and St. Michaels of Emmons County. He was at the latter about a year when he was assigned to Holy Trinity at Krassna from where he also seved St. Bernard's Mission church about 15 miles to the west. When he was assigned to Holy Trinity, he traded places with the Rev. John A. Selder, who is now pastor of St. Michael's church.

As far as is known, his mother and a sister still live in Czechoslovakia.

Msgr. William F. Garvin, vicar general of the Diocese of Bismarck, officated at funeral services held Monday morning at Holy Trinity Church. Arrangements were by the Kraft Funeral Home, Linton and burial was in the church cemetery.

Six former Czech-priests, from North Dakota and Canada, were pallbearers.

War

*This image of World War II rationing stamps and
books was provided by Airgroup 4, a dedicated
group of Naval Airmen who served in WWII.
airgroup4.com*

War

Dieser Krieg ist Schrecklich (This war is terrible) -
A quote from John Graf's Letter, 1943

Civilians played a big part in the war by serving in the military. The biggest part was the rationing of some very crucial commodities of almost everything used in daily living. The Office of Administration (OPA) was in charge of issuing ration books to every American, even babies. These books had a stamp with an expiration date. Each book was good for a month. This was done to prevent hoarding. Food items like sugar, coffee, butter, beef, and canned goods were each assigned a point value to be redeemed with ration stamps. Fortunately, the farmers did not have to buy butter. Since beef was in short supply, chickens raised on the farm were more available. A war slogan from Walter Winchell, a news commentator, was: "Roses are red, Violets are blue. Sugar is sweet. Remember?"

Another resource that was rationed was rubber. This made it nearly impossible to get tires for your car or machinery. In order to save rubber it was advised to drive less than 35 mph. A slogan from a radio personality was: "This is Fred Allen speaking for Texaco dealers from coast to coast reminding you to drive under 35 miles per hour to save rubber."

Gasoline for cars and machinery was also a rationed resource. This resulted in limited trips to town, which was only five to ten miles away. Windshield stickers indicated how many gallons you were allowed. Stickers with the letter "A" allowed the owner to get three to four gallons per week. Doctors and defense plant workers with jobs that required them to drive long distances were given "B" and "C" stickers. Truck drivers were also in that category. Some of stickers were counterfeit and sold on the black market. Many gas stations owners lost their licenses if they were part of the scam.

Life changed considerably during the war. Clothing styles

changed. Fabric such as nylon was used for making parachutes, so was not available for nylon stockings. The amount of fabric used for clothing was rationed. This caused the elimination of non-essential aspects of clothing such as cuffs, full skirts, wide hems, patch pockets and men's vests. Buttons were substituted for elastic for underwear.

Many new recipes appeared. The families learned to make pie and cake without sugar. Sometimes mayonnaise was substituted for cream or eggs. One time when my parents went to town, my brothers decided to make candy using up most of our sugar rations. My little sister and I were the receivers of that special treat. Can't remember what we got for punishment, maybe not being able to eat anything sweet for the rest of the month.

One farmer was so protective of his ration books that he carried them with him in his bib overalls pocket. Unfortunately, in bending over a machine the ration book fell out of his pocket into the machine and ended up being shredded. He had his whole family out in the field with a coffee can picking up all the little shreds.

Americans were also asked to grow their own food resulting in the Victory Gardens. The Germans From Russia, of course, had been doing this right along.

Another item that was hard to get was cigarettes. Although not rationed they were given free to the soldiers, leaving them in short supply for the civilians. Lucky Strike cigarettes changed their packaging from green to white because the metal being used for the green dye was needed for the war efforts.

Being German during the war not very cool and there was a lot of prejudice against anyone of German descent. This was particularly true in larger cities. Krassna was so isolated and almost everyone was G/R that they mostly escaped the intolerance.

A war slogan that was not new to G/R particularly in Krassna was "Use it up, wear it out, make it do, or do without."

After the war Krassna became much less isolated which changed the whole outlook of the people who lived there. Soldiers had traveled to places far away from Krassna. They were exposed to different foods and lifestyles. Some married girls from other parts of the country with nationalities different from the G/R. Electricity became available as well as running water. Phones also became available. The roads were more passable and with the availability of cars people were able to do more traveling. This was a cause for many changes, which created a broader outlook of a much larger world.

Emmons County Record
OFFICIAL NEWSPAPER OF EMMONS COUNTY AND CITY OF LINTON

1941

Sale of Health Stamps On Soon
School Children Will Again Have Charge of Sales In Emmons.

Opening next Monday, December 2, and continuing right up to the eve of Christmas the drive to sell Christmas seals in Emmons county will again be staged by school children under the supervision of the teachers.

Distribution of the seals is handled through the office of the county superintendent of schools. The supply of stamps will be given to teachers when they attend the county institute here tomorrow.

Proceeds from the sale of the seals go to fight tuberculosis. Camp Grassick, a haven for undernourished children, is maintained by money raised in this manner.

All of the money received from the sale of stamps stays in the state excepting about five cents of every dollar, which is the cost of printing. Half goes to the state tuberculosis society for use in the state and the other half remains here to help Emmons county children regain

their health Emmons county has set a good record in health seal

CHRISTMAS SEALS

sales in past years and the aim is to continue this fine showing in 1940.

1941

Military Highway
Designated Second In Priority is Proposed Network Of Strategic Highways

U.S. No 83 thru Emmons County may be made a part of a great national system of defense highways under a program submitted to President

Roosevelt recently.

Prepared by the Federal Public Works agency an appropriation of 287,000,000 has been asked by that group

to build a strategic network of military highways thruout the nation a measure deemed by the war Department to be of
Continued on next Page

Continued from Previous Page

first importance.

Under the plan, certain roads linking up important industrial centers and military locations would be given a first priority, others designated as important connecting links in the system would be given second priority. Group in the latter class is number 83. Connecting up with Canadian systems at the boundary it would run through North Dakota, connecting Bismarck and peer or South Dakota and on south to the golf according to tentative plans.

Designated as third priority or a certain access roads these being planned to connect main roads with army camps these would be the first to be built running from camps to the nearest

editorial Highway the Army would have almost exclusive right of weight on them. Federal funds would be used for new construction.

The state highway departments and votes administration would collaborate in the straightening of the strategic network under present plans with contributions to the improvement fund compulsory from the states although the federal contribution would be greater than the normal 5050 national a highway program.

Included in the bill is a provision for the reimbursement of any expenditures made by states and counties for repair of roads damaged by military use.

Required

improvements under the access road program range from resurfacing and widening of two-lane roads to the construction of multiple lane highways and large bridges. All of which would be completed in one year or less as possible, the report said.

The bulk of the appropriation would be earmarked for immediate construction of access roads to serve military and naval reservations and defense industries, and for immediate straightening of certain weak sections of the national highway system designated by the war and Navy departments as the strategic networks

5-19-1941

Hitler Marks 52nd Birthday at the Front

Berlin Germany was prepared for Adolf Hitler's 52nd birthday anniversary April 20 with a fanfare of proclamations hailing Nazi armed might and with an appeal from the dictator himself calling on the German people to grid themselves for a year of heavy combat and to increase donations for the care of war wounded.

Hitler was in the field at the head of his army of the Southeast. Hitler's proclamation declared "a heavy year of conflict stands before us."

In the German people's greatest struggle for it's political liberty and therefore its economic future and preservation of its life he said "this will go down in history as a great and memorable event."

Historic decisions of a unique scale will be made.

Since, however immeasurable demands once again are made on the men folk our people of the German homeland will be equally ready to make sacrifices.

I therefore renew the appeal to the German people to make voluntary donations to the second war relief work program of the Red Cross "thus giving the homeland's gift of best- care for the wounded and sick who have sacrificed themselves for their people as the best soldiers in the world."

1-8-1942

Tire Rationing Board Is Named
County Defense Counsel Selects Mrs.Hogue, Lenhart And Ray Bichler

On orders from the state defense office, J.D. Meier, chairman of the Emmons County Defense council called a meeting of that organization Friday evening to name and select a tire rationing board for the county. Mrs. Kathryn Hogue, Linton was named chairman, to act with G.A. Lenhart, Hazelton, and Ray Bichler, Strasburg.

Regulations concerning the rationing of tires went into effect January 5, and from now on persons desiring to purchase tires may do so only thru contacting the rationing board. The board will be charged with four general duties. They are to determine eligibility to buy tires under regulations of the office of Price Administration: issues certificates permitting purchase of tires maintain records of applications issued and denied; and make periodic reports to the state defense counsel.

Continued on next Page

Continued from Previous Page

At present the plan is to set up an office in the city hall in Linton. The WPA, it is understood, will supply secretaries for the chairman. The board may meet once a week to act on applications, but this is not certain until further orders are received.

As we understand it, the average motorist has no chance to get new tires. Those who are eligible, as announced some time ago, are operators of vehicles used exclusively in protection of public health and safety or for essential freight and bus transportation or industrial and commercial operations.

The regulations provide that purchase certificates for new tires may not be issued unless an applicant certifies that the tires or tubes bought "will be mounted" on:

1- vehicles used by physicians, surgeons, visiting nurses and veterinarians, principally for professional services.

1942

Emmons County to Get 29 Tires in January

Emmons County motorists and truckers will be limited to 16 tires and 13 inner tubes for all kinds of vehicles including passenger cars, trucks and buses during January, under quotas announced last week in the first wartime rationing of tires.

The allotment for passenger cars is six tires and five tubes and for trucks and buses 10 tires and 6 tubes. The rationing of tires is placed in the hands of a County Board which will determine to whom tires shall go.

Billings and Slope counties are limited to one tire and one tube for passenger cars for the month and Sioux and Billings are limited to two tires and two tubes for trucks and buses

Emmons County Record

1942
Drive for War Funds Progressing
Many Chairmen Report Quotas Reached; January 11 in Red Cross Sunday

Progress marked the first week of the campaign to raise Emmons County's share of a $50 million emergency war funds for the American Red Cross with indications that the County's quota of $1,500 would soon be subscribed.

While no figures were yet available, Harry C. Lynn, head of the county drive, reported that several of the Committee Chairman of the various communities had advised their quotas had been reached.

One-third of the county's quotas is to be raised in Linton and surrounding territory. The Strasburg community is asked to contribute $200. Hague $125, Hull $50, Westfield $50 Winona $50, Temvik, Braddock and Kintyre $125 each,, Hazelton community $250.

At the request of chapters thruout the nation, next Sunday, January 11 has been designated as "Red Cross Sunday" in the hope that every pulpit in America will be an interpreter of those eternal varieties.

1942
State-Wide Scrap Metal Salvage Drives Soon

An intensive state-wide salvage drive for the reclamation of scrap metal will be staged in North Dakota between September 19 and October 19, according E. E. Campion, state salvage director.

"Our plans call for scrap gathering agencies in every city and village in the state," he says. "County salvage committees will be enlarged so as to include implement dealers, oil station operators, automobile dealers and tire shop men. Newspapermen and other professional people will also be asked to join the committee in this, the most intensive drive ever staged in North Dakota."

City village and township salvage committees will be on the job and see to it that every pound of scrap metal is brought to town during this drive, according to Mr. Campion.

Implement dealers will supervise the campaign in the farming communities, and automobile oil and tire dealers will handle the drive in cities and villages" Campion states.

Emmons County Record

1942

Sugar Stamp 8 Good for 5 pounds
To cover Ten-Weeks Period Beginning August 23

Sugar ration stamp number eight will be good for five pounds of sugar in the ten-weeks period beginning August 23 and ending October 31 the office of Price administration in Washington announced Saturday.

While not changing the basic ration of 1/2 pound per person per week it will enable the consumers to make purchase in larger units and facilitate the disposal of five, ten and 25 pound packages.

Packages of these sizes were put up before the start of rationing and processors have had difficulty marketing any substantial part of them because ration stamps to date have been good for one or two--pound purchases. Unless this sugar is sold, the OPA said it would be repacked, causing an "undesirable waste of labor and materials."

Stamps number six and seven, each good for two pounds of sugar, may be used until midnight this week Saturday, August 22. Stamp number seven gave the consumer a two-pound bonus.

1942

Coffee Drinkers Must Cut to Cup a Day

Coffee drinkers of the nation will be required to cut down their daily ration to about a cup a day when the new rationing goes into effect at midnight November 28 according to the order of price administrator Leon Henderson. This of course includes the people of Emmons County and will work somewhat of a hardship on those businessmen of Linton and other Emmons towns who have acquired the habit of drinking there afternoon cup of coffee.

The rationing will be on the basis of 1 pound each five weeks -about a cup a day- for all persons who were 15 years old or older when they registered for sugar supplies on May 4-5 All retail sales of coffee will be frozen at midnight November 21, for the week before rationing begins in order to allow merchants to stock their shelves.

Consumers will not have to register to obtain coffee;they will uses their sugar rationing books. To get the first coffee ration the consumer will be required to surrender the last stamp number 28 in the sugar book. Subsequent ration of coffee will be coupons taken in sequence.

Emmons County Record

1944

Children Gather Milkweed Floss

The schoolchildren of North Dakota are being praised for their cooperation in the collection of milk weed, says. Thompson, state superintendent of public instruction. The fiber is secured for the manufacture of life jackets and flying suits for the Armed Forces. The floss collected by schoolchildren particularly in the eastern part of the state were milk weed grows in greater abundance are dried and turned over to county war boards before shipment to processing plants.

1944

Tin Cans Are Badly Needed
More Tin is Needed for Use in Almost Every War Maneuver

The war effort is progressing nicely but there is one thing that can hinder this progress that we folks no matter where we may be can do something about. That is a shortage of tin which is used for practically every war operation, from getting food, weapons and medical supplies to the boys, to actually being part of the shells, guns, tanks and other equipment which they use.

The folks at home can help in providing as much as possible to the soldiers and sailors by saving all the tin cans we have, washing them and turning them into the salvage depots. The proper method of preparation of the cans is to wash them, cut the ends out, flattened them with the ends inside. Then they can be saved and when a collection of this material is made the cans should be turned in.

The serious need of saving all the tin cans can be realized when it is remembered that in normal times 90% of the tin we used in this country came from countries now in Japanese hands. Until that territory is regained and production of tin cans can be resumed the most of the tin that is needed for the war effort will have to come from our own country and a good percentage of that from the tin cans you and I save. Start today to save your cans and when a drive is made have them ready to contribute.

The next collection in Linton will be early October.

Epilogue

If you listen carefully you can hear the wind whispering about all the hardships, the joys and the sorrows of these German from Russia immigrants who settled here so many years ago. The wind still blows the tumble weeds across the windswept prairie and the gophers still scamper to their holes. The meadowlarks still sing. The sun dogs fade with the dawn of a new day.

One school is left standing with its loose hinges flipping back and forth with the wind blowing through the broken glass. The other schools are now gone, their parts used for granaries, torn down.

The church was torn down after standing empty for many years. No funds were available for its massive restoration and the store disappeared long ago.

The cemetery still holds the ghosts of our ancestors.

The students who could barely speak English now have offspring scattered across the world. They are business people, teachers, professors, doctors, dentists, politicians, farmers and other professionals. The place is no longer the same. Super highways and corporate farms have replaced the prairie community and Krassna is no more.

Author

Angie Reinbold Ibarra was born in Krassna, North Dakota and lived all her formative years in South Dakota. She has called California, New York, Texas, Washington, D.C. and now Minnesota home. Angie attended the University of Minnesota and graduated from Metropolitan State University. She is a former flight attendant, homemaker, Substitute Teacher for the St. Paul, Minnesota public high schools, a Licensed Private Detective, previous owner of her own Private Detective Agency and employer of Security Guards. Today, Angie is employed as a private detective for ADP, Inc., an international company specializing in background checks. Her previous writings appeared in the Stillwater Gazette. Stillwater, MN. She currently lives with her husband in Vadnais Heights.

Angie Ibarra
email: Krassna@q.com

Elsie Pool (Ryckman) my 4th grade teacher.
When I started writng this book I wondered if Elsie Pool still lived in the
area. I found an address for her and wrote a letter asking if she was the
person who taught at the Krassna school. She wrote back and said she was.
On a trip to South Dakota I stopped to visit her and we had our picture taken.